The NEW BIG BOOK of LOGOS

David E. Carter
editor

book design
Suzanna M.W.

layout & production
Graham Allen
Christa Carter

The New Big Book of Logos

First published in 2000 by HBI,
an imprint of HarperCollins Publishers
10 East 53rd Street
New York, NY 10022-5299

ISBN: 0688-17890-1

Distributed in the U.S. and Canada by
Watson-Guptill Publications
1515 Broadway
New York, NY 10036
Tel: (800) 451-1741
        (732) 363-4511 in NJ, AK, HI
Fax: (732) 363-0338

Distributed throughout the rest of the world by
HarperCollins International
10 East 53rd Street
New York, NY 10022-5299
Fax: (212) 207-7654

First published in Germany by Nippan
Nippon Shuppan Hanbai
Deutschland GmbH
Krefelder Strasse 85
D-40549 Dusseldorf
Tel: (0211) 5048089
Fax: (0211) 5049326
nippan@t-online.de

ISBN: 3-931884-71-6

Printed in Hong Kong by Everbest Printing Company
through Four Colour Imports, Louisville, Kentucky.

Once upon a time, there was a big book.

A **Big Book of Logos**. It became a major seller. Well, not by John Grisham or Stephen King standards, but in the world of graphics, it was huge. It actually cracked the circle of the top 3% of ALL books sold on Amazon.com.

Graphic designers really, really liked this book. And when a book is that successful, **you know what happens**: a sequel.

So, the publishers huffed, and they puffed, and they convinced David Carter to do another Big Book of Logos. (He wanted to call the book "Green Eggs and Ham", but that title was already taken.) **THIS is THAT book**.

And, oh yes, they reminded him that this sequel had to be just as good as—or better than—the original. Someone said something about "an offer you can't turn down."

We listened carefully, and selected about 2,500 outstanding logos that had been designed in the last three years. And, once again, **The NEW Big Book of Logos** will go into the design world and say "We've done it again."

This book, combined with its predecessor, contains well over 5,000 great logo designs. This may be one of the best sources of logo design ideas ever assembled. (Or maybe not. That's for you to judge. But we think you'll find this great collection to be inspirational.)

To paraphrase W.P. Kinsella, "Publish it and they will buy."

David E. Carter

1.

PRETTY GOOD PRIVACY™

2.

avenue a™

3.

ALTA

4.

ATRÉVA™

5.

Charter
COMMUNICATIONS®

6.

A WIRED WORLD COMPANY

blue nile

7.

grape finds℠

8.

9.

SAVIshopper.com

STEWART CAPITAL MANAGEMENT

10.

11.

innoVentry™

12.

13.

mc²

14.

healthshop.com

MODULAR TECHNOLOGY

15.

(all)

Design Firm   Hornall Anderson Design Works

1. Client   Best Cellars
    Designers   Jack Anderson, Lisa Cerveny,
                     Jana Wilson Esser, David Bates,
                     & Nicole Bloss

2. Client   (PGP) Pretty Good Privacy
    Designers   Jack Anderson, Debra
                     McCloskey, Michael Brugman,
                     Heidi Favour, Jana Wilson Esser,
                     & Katha Dalton

3. Client   Avenue A
    Designers   Jack Anderson, Debra
                     McCloskey, Tobi Brown,
                     Henry Yiu, James Tee,
                     & Gretchen Cook

4. Client   Alta Beverage Company
    Designers   Jack Anderson, Larry Anderson,
                     & Julie Keenan

5. Client   Wells Fargo "Atreva"
    Designers   Jack Anderson, Kathy Saito,
                     Alan Copeland, Cliff Chung,
                     & Chris Sallquist

6. Client   Charter Communications
    Designers   Jack Anderson, Lisa Cerveny,
                     Jana Wilson Esser, Mike Calkins,
                     David Bates, Julia LaPine,
                     & Sonja Max

7. Client   Blue Nile
    Designers   Jack Anderson, Bruce Stigler,
                     Gretchen Cook, Henry Yiu,
                     & Sonja Max

8. Client   grapefinds
    Designers   Jack Anderson, Lisa Cerveny,
                     Gretchen Cook, Jana Wilson
                     Esser, & Mary Chin Hutchison

9. Client   SaviShopper.com
    Designers   Jack Anderson, Ryan Wilkerson,
                     Naomi Davidson
                     & Margaret Long

10. Client   Stewart Capital Management
    Designers   Jack Anderson, Debra
                     McCloskey, David Bates,
                     & Lisa Cerveny

11. Client   Wells Fargo "innoVentry"
    Designers   Jack Anderson, Kathy Saito,
                     Sonja Max, & Alan Copeland

12. Client   (RPM) Wells Fargo
    Designers   Jack Anderson, Kathy Saito,
                     Sonja Max, & Alan Copeland

13. Client   MC²
    Designers   Jack Anderson & Margaret Long

14. Client   Healthshop.com
    Designers   Jack Anderson, Mary Hermes,
                     Mike Calkins, David Bates,
                     & Holly Finlayson

15. Client   K2 Corporation
    Designers   Jack Anderson, Andrew Smith,
                     Taro Sakita, & Mary Chin
                     Hutchison

1.

2.

3.

OUTDOOR SERVICES

4.

The Internet Passport Company

5.

BroadStream

6.

VARNA
PLATINUM

7.

MORPHEUS
MUSIC

8.

9.

10.

TRADITION BANK

11.

12.

13.

14.

15.

1
  Design Firm   **Sayles Graphic Design**
2 - 10
  Design Firm   **Glyphix Studio**
11 - 15
  Design Firm   **The Focus Group**

1. Client   Phil Goode Grocery
    Designer   John Sayles

2. Client   The Jewish Federation/
              Valley Alliance
    Designer   Paul Ruettgers

3. Client   USA Loan
    Designer   Brad Wilder

4. Client   Outdoor Services
    Designer   Brad Wilder

5. Client   HotBrowse
    Designer   Brad Wilder

6. Client   Broadstream
    Designer   Brad Wilder

7. Client   Varna Platinum
    Designer   Brad Wilder

8. Client   Morpheus Music
    Designer   Brad Wilder

9. Client   City of Los Angeles
    Designer   Brad Wilder

10. Client   eSpine
     Designers   Eric Sena & Brad Wilder

11. Client   Tradition Bank
     Designer   Kirk Davis

12. Client   TeleCheck
     Designers   Dan Feder & Kelly Johnson

13. Client   Loomis, Fargo & Co.
     Designer   Kirk Davis

14. Client   Houston Postal Credit Union
     Designer   Kelly Johnson

15. Client   Solvay Polymers
     Designer   Kelly Johnson

1.

2.

3.

DEEP ELLUM DASH

4.

5.

DEEP ELLUM

6.

7.

1 - 7
Design Firm Squires & Company

1. Client   Uptown Run, Annual 5K,
                     10K Run
    Designer   Christie Grotheim

2. Client   DECA Art Gallery
                     Featuring Local Artists
    Designer   Christie Grotheim

3. Client   Deep Ellum Dash '97
                     10K Fun Run
    Designer   Paul Black

4. Client   Aqua Star, Pools and Spa
    Designer   Paul Black

5. Client   Deep Ellum Association
                     An Historic Industrial
                     Area of Dallas
    Designer   Paul Black

6. Client   Communigroup
    Designers   Amy Chang & Brandon Murphy

7. Client   Sushi Nights, Restaurant and Bar
    Designer   Christie Grotheim

(opposite)
Design Firm Dixon & Parcels Associates, Inc.

    Client   Eggland's Best, Inc.

CYBERLIBRARIANS.COM

1.

YOKIBICS

MINDBODY FITNESS
FOR TODAY'S
SPIRITUAL WARRIOR

2.

POWER
TRAVEL

3.

KITCHENS
by
DESIGN

4.

SOUL
MIND BODY HEART

5.

earth
Medicine
inc

6.

heather

7.

You
deserve
great
legs

Dr. Julius W. Garvey

8.

10

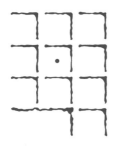

mark d. bennett, cpa

9.

WILSON
COMMUNICATIONS
INTEGRATED TELEPHONE SOLUTIONS

10.

ADVANCED**TRAINING**
SOLUTIONS

11.

Transpro

12.

REMMY'S
CAFE · DELI · CATERING

13.

NISQUALLY MEADOWS

14.

TAMBAR

15.

1 - 8
Design Firm   Guarino Graphics
& Design Studio

9 - 15
Design Firm   Graphic Technologies

1.	Client	Cyberlibrarians.com	8.	Client	Dr. Julius Garvey
	Designer	Jan Guarino		Designer	Jan Guarino
2.	Client	Yokibics	9.	Client	Mark Bennett, CPA
	Designer	Jan Guarino		Designer	Gary Thompson
3.	Client	Power Travel	10.	Client	Wilson Communications
	Designer	Jan Guarino		Designer	Gary Thompson
4.	Client	Kitchens by Design	11.	Client	Advanced Training Solutions
	Designer	Jan Guarino		Designer	Gary Thompson
5.	Client	Soul•Mind•Body•Heart	12.	Client	Transpro
	Designer	Jan Guarino		Designer	Gary Thompson
6.	Client	Earth Medicine	13.	Client	Remmy's
	Designer	Jan Guarino		Designer	Gary Thompson
7.	Client	Heather	14.	Client	Nisqually
	Designer	Jan Guarino		Designer	Gary Thompson
			15.	Client	Tambar
				Designer	Gary Thompson

1.

2.

3.

Wesley Village

4.

HAUTe DECOR •COM

5.

Interactive Brand Center

6.

7.

8.

eventra

9.

10.

11.

12.

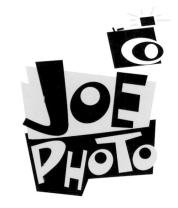

13.

NETWORK

SOCIETY™ 14.

THE RIDGE
COMMUNITY CHURCH

15.

1 - 8
Design Firm Tom Fowler, Inc.
9, 12, 14
Design Firm Edmonds Design
10, 11, 13
Design Firm Fuse, Inc.
15
Design Firm Graphic Technologies

1. Client   Ross Products Division/
                    Abbott Laboratories
    Designer   Thomas G. Fowler

2. Client   St. Luke's LifeWorks
    Designer   Karl S. Maruyama

3. Client   Reynolds and Rose
    Designer   Karl S. Maruyama

4. Client   United Methodist Homes
    Designers   Thomas G. Fowler
                    & Karl S. Maruyama

5. Client   Haute Decor.com
    Designers   Thomas G. Fowler
                    & Elizabeth P. Ball

6. Client   IBC
    Designer   Elizabeth P. Ball

7. Client   Ocean Fox Dive Shop
    Designer   Thomas G. Fowler

8. Client   Eventra
    Designer   Karl S. Maruyama

9. Client   Network Computing Magazine
    Designer   Nancy Edmonds

10. Client   Fuse, Inc.
    Designer   Russell Pierce

11. Client   PairGain—StarGazer
    Designer   Russell Pierce

12. Client   Mac Publishing/MacWorld
    Designer   Nancy Edmonds

13. Client   Joe Photo
    Designer   Russell Pierce

14. Client   Network Computing Magazine
    Designer   Nancy Edmonds

15. Client   The Ridge Community Church
    Designer   Gary Thompson

Chesebrough-Pond's USA Co.

LYNX

ARTWORK TRANSFER SYSTEM

1.

directfit
we get IT.

2.

centricity

3.

pairgain
THE POWER OF DSL ACCESS

4.

5.

6.

7.

1
Design Firm Tom Fowler, Inc.
2 - 6
Design Firm Fuse, Inc.
7
Design Firm Squires & Company

1. Client	Chesebrough-Ponds USA Co	
Designer	Elizabeth P. Ball	
2. Client	DirectFit	
Designers	Matthew Stainner & Mike Esperanza	
3. Client	Centricity	
Designer	Russell Pierce	
4. Client	PairGain	
Designer	Mike Esperanza	

5. Client	Taco Bell—Nothing Ordinary About It
Designer	Russell Pierce
6. Client	Yamaha Corporation of America
Designer	Kristi Kamei
7. Client	I Think, Inc.
Designers	Clark Bystrom & Paul Black

(opposite)
Design Firm Miriello Grafico Inc.

Client	Eastpack
Designer	Ron Miriello

K I D **C** ONCEPTS

1.

MARTHA

ROEDIGER

2.

tom mcpherson

PHOTOGRAPHY

3.

HIGH ROAD

4.

ENTERIX

5.

MIND STEP

Creations

6.

ASSET
PR TECTION
ASSOCIATES

PROTECTING WHAT YOU HAVE EARNED

FOR THE REST OF YOUR LIFE

7.

TECHNIUM

8.

The *Rory* David Deutsch
F O U N D A T I O N
*Brighter Tomorrows for Children
With Brain Tumors*

9.

CONSULTING SERVICES

10.

GEORGE ORLOFF, M.D.

11.

12.

MACGUFFIN
management

13.

14.

15.

1 - 6
Design Firm Thibault Paolini
Design Associates

7 - 10
Design Firm Design Moves, Ltd.

11 - 12
Design Firm Glyphix Studio

13 - 15
Design Firm Squires & Company

1. Client   Kid Concepts
Designers Renée Fournier
& Sue Schenning

2. Client   Martha Roediger
Designer Renée Fournier

3. Client   Tom McPherson Photography
Designer Renée Fournier

4. Client   Talus
Designer Sue Schenning

5. Client   Enterix
Designers Judy Paolini & Sue Schenning

6. Client   Mind Step Creations
Designer Sue Schenning

7. Client   Asset Protection Associates
Designers Laurie Freed, Bill Sprowl,
& Jennifer Rayburn

8. Client   Technium, Inc.
Designers Laurie Freed, Bill Sprowl,
& Jennifer Rayburn

9. Client   Rory David Deutsch Foundation
Designers Laurie Medeiros Freed,
Eric Halloran, Jennifer Rayburn,
& Bill Sprowl

10. Client   Information Management
Group
Designers Laurie Freed, Jennifer Rayburn,
Bill Sprowl, & Amy Forbes

11. Client   George Orloff, M.D.
Designer Eric Sena

12. Client   ResourceLink
Designer Eric Sena

13. Client   MacGuffin
Designer Christie Grotheim

14. Client   Deep Ellum Arts Festival
Designers Thomas Vasquez & Paul Black

15. Client   Jenson
Designer Paul Black

**Palo Alto
Recycling
Program**

1.

GreenPeas
CATERING

2.

KIND OF
LOUD
TECHNOLOGIES

3.

Palo Alto
Festival
of the Arts

UNIVERSITY AVE.

4.

**KEYS
SCHOOL**

5.

Trinity School

6.

7.

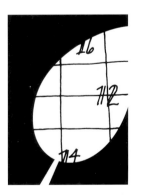

8.

redwing™

9.

NOVALIS™

10.

MAYDAY
PEDIATRIC HEADACHE
CENTER ℠

11.

COSMETIC SURGERY CENTER
OF LANCASTER ℠

at Lancaster General Hospital Health Campus

12.

13.

DA

technology
solutions, LLC

14.

HISTORIC

ROCK·FORD
PLANTATION

15.

1.

2.

3.

4.

5.

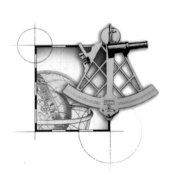

6.

7.

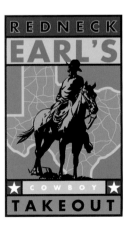

8.

20

CORTANA

9.

THE
STANFORD
FUND

10.

WEBCOR
DESIGN • BUILD

11.

WEBCOR
I • C • G

12.

SUSQUEHANNA
ADDICTIONS CENTER

13.

HIGHLANDS
AT WARWICK

14.

15.

1, 3, 4
Design Firm Ross West Design
2, 5, 6
Design Firm GA Design
7 - 12
Design Firm Artefact Design
13 - 15
**Design Firm Albert/Bogner Design
            Communications**

1. Client	Dr. Andrew J. Kapust DDS
Designer	Ross West
2. Client	Microsoft
Designer	Ross West
3. Client	Ross West Design
Designer	Ross West
4. Client	Microsoft
Designer	Ross West
5. Client	Washington Mutual
Designer	Ross West
6. Client	Microsoft
Designer	Ross West
7. Client	Joe's 40th Birthday
Designer	Kim Schwede

8. Client	Redneck Earl's Cowboy Takeout
Designer	Artefact Design
9. Client	Cortana Corporation
Designers	Artefact Design, Kim Schwede
10. Client	The Stanford Fund
Designer	Artefact Design
11. Client	Webcor Builders, Inc.
Designer	Artefact Design
12. Client	Webcor Builders, Inc.
Designer	Artefact Design
13. Client	Susquehanna Addictions Center
Designers	Kelly Albert & Marie Elaina Miller
14. Client	Highlands at Warwick
Designer	Kelly Albert
15. Client	Quarryville Retirement Community
Designers	Kelly Albert & Marie Elaina Miller

 **UniSource Energy**

1.

 **DakotaCom.net**

2.

certified organic

Boxed Greens

farm fresh • home delivery

3.

West by Southwest Entertainment

4.

SUN CITY VISTOSO COMMUNITY FOUNDATION

5.

Best **Mortgage** Finders, Inc.

The best source for your home loan.

6.

welcome back   about us   our portfolio

7.

aire

8.

22

9.

Favorite Childhood Originals for Infants & Toddlers

10.

Planet Waves

world music festival '99

11.

12.

13.

14.

15.

1 - 12			8. Client	aire design company
Design Firm	**aire design company**		Designers	Catharine Kim
13 - 15				& Daniel Morrison
Design Firm	**Sayles Graphic Design**			
			9. Client	Mi Hijito, L.L.C.
1. Client	Unisource Energy		Designer	Catharine Kim
Designers	Catharine Kim, Matthew Rivera,			
	& Shari Rykowski		10. Client	Mi Hijito, L.L.C.
			Designer	Catharine Kim
2. Client	DakotaCom.net			
Designers	Matthew Rivera		11. Client	West by Southwest
	& Catharine Kim			Entertainment
			Designer	Catharine Kim
3. Client	Boxed Greens			
Designers	Catharine Kim		12. Client	Solutions
	& Shari Rykowski		Designers	Helene Upson & Catharine Kim
4. Client	West by Southwest		13. Client	Meredith Corporation
	Entertainment			Successful Farming:
Designer	Catharine Kim			Crunch Time
			Designer	John Sayles
5. Client	Sun City Vistoso			
Designers	Catharine Kim		14. Client	Meredith Corporation
	& Matthew Rivera			Successfu. Farming:
				Industrial Revolution
6. Client	Best Mortgage Finders, Inc.		Designer	John Sayles
Designer	Shari Rykowski			
			15. Client	Chicago Tribune
7. Client	aire design company			"Chicago's Choice"
Designer	Catharine Kim		Designer	John Sayles

HORVATH
DESIGN
GRAPHIC DESIGN, LOGOS
& FINE HAND LETTERING

1.

FOOT
&
ANKLE
ASSOCIATES
DECATUR · BLUFFTON
219-724-7179 219-824-2212

2.

Baggerie
K A N S A S   C I T Y

3.

DREAM
HOME
ADVISOR

4.

Singer's

5.

kitchenthink
C R E A T I V E   C O N S U L T I N G

6.

HARRINGTON
DEVELOPMENT
I N C.

7.

MULTI
GRAPHICS ™

8.

24

OMAN

9.

ENNISKNUPP

10.

*i*Believe.com℠
Christian Faith in Everyday Life

11.

*i*flourish℠
My Active Living Resource

12.

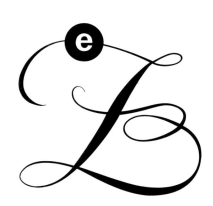

13.

14.

15.

1 - 7
Design Firm Horvath Design
8 - 14
Design Firm Liska + Associates, Inc.
15
Design Firm Sayles Graphic Design

1. Client	Horvath Design	
Designer	Kevin Horvath	
2. Client	Foot & Ankle Clinic	
Designer	Kevin Horvath	
3. Client	Baggerie	
Designer	Kevin Horvath	
4. Client	Dream Home Advisor	
Designer	Kevin Horvath	
5. Client	Singers Restaurant	
Designer	Kevin Horvath	
6. Client	Kitchen Think	
Designer	Kevin Horvath	
7. Client	Harrington Development	
Designer	Kevin Horvath	

8. Client	Multigraphics
Designer	Andrea Wener
9. Client	Oman Photography
Designer	Steve Liska
10. Client	EnnisKnupp & Associates
Designer	Liska + Associates, Inc.
11. Client	iBelieve.com
Designer	Liska + Associates, Inc.
12. Client	iFlourish.com
Designer	Liska + Associates, Inc.
13. Client	Elizabeth Zeschin Photography
Designer	Bonnie Giard
14. Client	Reptile Artists Agents
Designer	Holle Andersen
15. Client	Patee Enterprises "Hometown Christmas"
Designer	John Sayles

1.

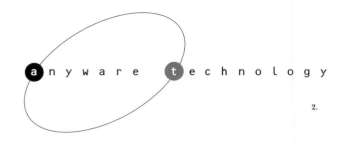

2.

3.

4.

5.

6.

7.

1 - 9
Design Firm Squires & Company

1. Client   Populi
    Designers   Brandon Murphy & Amy Chang

2. Client   Anyware Technology
    Designer   Brandon Murphy

3. Client   Pro Color Imaging
    Designers   Kristine Murphy
                 & Brandon Murphy

4. Client   Loomis Productions
    Designer   Kristine Murphy

5. Client   Black Rhino Graphics
    Designers   Kristine Murphy
                 & Brandon Murphy

6. Client   Hill Country Equestrian Lodge
    Designers   Bryan Hynecek
                 & Brandon Murphy

7. Client   Moving Pictures Editorial
    Designers   Kristine Murphy
                 & Brandon Murphy

(opposite)
Design Firm Squires & Company

8. Client   Deep Ellum Dash '98,
                 Annual Fun Run
    Designer   Christie Grotheim

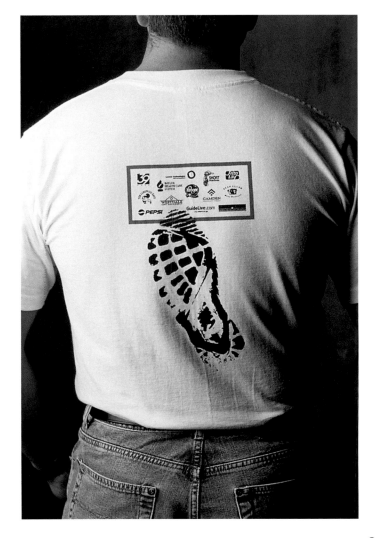

SHAMAN

Good Medicine For Technology

1.

info
WORKS

2.

accompany

3.

SOHO
ρROVISIONS

4.

VERGE
SOFTWARE

5.

PULSENT

Technology for the new media experience.

6.

Qualify

7.

Just Give
.org

8.

9.

10.

11.

12.

13.

14.

15.

1 - 8
Design Firm Diesel Design
9 - 15
Design Firm Macnab Design
         Visual Communication

1. Client	Shaman	8. Client	Just Give.org
Designer	Amy Bainbridge	Designers	Amy Bainbridge
			& Luis Dominguez

1.	Client	Shaman
	Designer	Amy Bainbridge

2. Client Info Works
   Designer Aaron Morton

3. Client Accompany
   Designer Aaron Morton

4. Client Soho Provisions
   Designer Pam Purser

5. Client Verge Software
   Designer Luis Dominguez

6. Client Pulsent
   Designer Luis Dominguez

7. Client iQualify
   Designer Heather Bodlak

8. Client Just Give.org
   Designers Amy Bainbridge
   & Luis Dominguez

9. Client Samba
   Designer Maggie Macnab

10. Client Truchas Hydrologic Associates
    Designer Maggie Macnab

11. Client Swan Songs
    Designer Maggie Macnab

12. Client MUSE Technologies Inc.
    Designer Maggie Macnab

13. Client CSI Technologies Inc.
    Designer Maggie Macnab

14. Client Heart Hospital of New Mexico
    Designer Maggie Macnab

15. Client Oriental Medicine Consultants
    Designer Maggie Macnab

1.

2.

3.

4.

5.

6.

7.

8.

9.

Entercom

Marketing

Resource

Group

10.

11.

12.

13.

14.

Michael Luis & Associates

15.

1 - 15			
Design Firm	**Art O Mat Design**		
		8. Client	Pryor Giggey Co.
1. Client	Technology Alliance	Designers	Jacki McCarthy
Designers	Jacki McCarthy		& Mark Kaufman
	& Mark Kaufman		
		9. Client	Entercom Marketing
2. Client	Seattle Symphony—Wolfgang		Resource Group
Designers	Jacki McCarthy	Designers	Jacki McCarthy
	& Mark Kaufman		& Mark Kaufman
3. Client	107.7 The End—Step Right Up	10. Client	Indigo Springs
Designers	Jacki McCarthy	Designers	Jacki McCarthy
	& Mark Kaufman		& Mark Kaufman
4. Client	107.7 The End—Endfest 3	11. Client	Seattle Symphony—
Designers	Jacki McCarthy		Make a Sound Downtown
	& Mark Kaufman	Designers	Jacki McCarthy
			& Mark Kaufman
5. Client	107.7 The End—Endfest 1		
Designers	Jacki McCarthy	12. Client	Mens Room
	& Mark Kaufman	Designers	Jacki McCarthy
			& Mark Kaufman
6. Client	107.7 The End—		
	Deck the Hall Ball	13. Client	Seattle Symphony—Nightingale
Designers	Jacki McCarthy	Designers	Jacki McCarthy
	& Mark Kaufman		& Mark Kaufman
7. Client	Seattle Symphony—	14. Client	Predict Navigator
	Musically Speaking	Designers	Jacki McCarthy
Designers	Jacki McCarthy		& Mark Kaufman
	& Mark Kaufman		
		15. Client	Michael Luis & Associates
		Designers	Jacki McCarthy
			& Mark Kaufman

1.

2.

Chambers
Cable

3.

Chambers
PRODUCTIONS

4.

All Women's
HEALTH SERVICES

5.

into
CAREERS

6.

PARK 5

BISTRO

7.

1 - 7
Design Firm Funk and Associates

1. Client   Stephanie Pearl Kimmel
    Designer   Beverly Soasey

2. Client   Café Yumm
    Designer   Christopher Berner

3. Client   Chambers
                Communication, Copp.
    Designers   Kathleen Heinz, Christopher
                Berner, & David Funk

4. Client   Chambers
                Communication, Copp.
    Designers   Kathleen Heinz, Christopher
                Berner, & David Funk

5. Client   All Women's Health Services
    Designer   Joan Gilbert Madsen

6. Client   Career Information System
    Designers   Beverly Soasey
                & Kathleen Heinz

7. Client   Epping
    Designer   Beverly Soasey

(opposite)
Design Firm Pace Design Group

    Client   Providian Financial Corporation
    Designer   Evan Deterling

1.

Cinnabar Hills
Golf Club

H

HAMPTON FINANCIAL PARTNERS

2.

INFINET
INCORPORATED

3.

VERIDA

4.

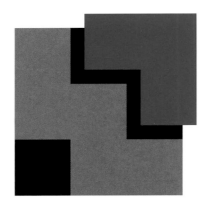

5.

Point Connect

6.

7.

1
Design Firm Bauer Holland Design

3
Design Firm Cathey Associates, Inc.

2, 4 - 7
Design Firm Triad, Inc.

1. Client   Cinnabar Hills Golf Club
    Designers   Julie Holland & Suzanne Bauer

2. Client   Hampton Financial Partners
    Designer   Michael Dambrowski

3. Client   InfiNet, Inc.
    Designer   Gordon Cathey

4. Client   Verida Internet Corp.
    Designer   Diana Kollanyi

5. Client   PointConnect Inc.
    Designer   Michael Dambrowski

6. Client   PointConnect Inc.
    Designer   Diana Kollanyi

7. Client   PointConnect Inc.
    Designer   Michael Dambrowski

(opposite)
Design Firm Donovan and Green

    Client   Faroy
    Designers   Janet Johnson & Ryan Paul

FAROY

M@llNet™

1.

Custom Rug Design

2.

PRO**TAB**

3.

Communications, Inc.

4.

state of mind

5.

6.

LE⌃P

7.

**Connecting
Global Life Science**

8.

36

ATCC

9.

electric stock

10.

Jet Silver

11.

gREPTILE GRIP

12.

the **inferno** sound room

13.

The **FIREHOUSE**

14.

★ **O**
OUTRIGGER™

15.

1
Design Firm Donovan and Green
2 - 4
Design Firm Cathey Associates, Inc.
5 - 7
Design Firm Desgrippes Gobé
8 - 10
Design Firm Stephen Loges Graphic Design
11 - 15
Design Firm Phoenix Creative

1. Client   MallNet
   Designer   Janet Johnson

2. Client   Unifications
   Designer   Gordon Cathey

3. Client   ProTab
   Designer   Gordon Cathey

4. Client   One Source
                 Communications, Inc.
   Designer   Matt Westapher

5. Client   CBI Laboratory
   Designers   Susan Berson & Deirdre Tighe

6. Client   Unisunstar B.V., Inc.
   Designers   Phyllis Aragaki & Deirdre Tighe

7. Client   Leap Energy and Power Corp.
   Designers   Phyllis Aragaki & Natalie Jacobs

8. Client   BioNexus Foundation
   Designer   Stephen Loges

9. Client   ATCC
   Designer   Stephen Loges

10. Client   Electric Stock
    Designer   Stephen Loges

11. Client   Edison Brothers Stores (5•7•9)
    Designer   Danielle John

12. Client   Pearl Izumi/Greptile Grip
    Designer   Steve Wienke

13. Client   The Inferno Sound Room
    Designer   Kathy Wilkinson

14. Client   The Firehouse
    Designer   Kathy Wilkinson

15. Client   Edison Brothers Stores/
                 Outrigger
    Designer   Jenny Anderson

1.

2.

3.

4.

5.

6.

7.

(opposite)

Design Firm	**Sayles Graphic Design**		3. Client	Cracker Barrel Old Country Store/Back Porch
Client	2000 Iowa State Fair "Zero In On Fun"		Designer	Kathy Wilkinson
Designer	John Sayles		4. Client	Cracker Barrel Old Country Store (Tea Set)
1 - 7			Designer	Curtis Potter
Design Firm	**Phoenix Creative**		5. Client	Borders/Living Through Books
1. Client	Borders/Youth Poetry Slam		Designer	Kathy Wilkinson
Designers	Deborah Finkelstein & Jenny Anderson		6. Client	The Spotted Dog Café
			Designer	Kathy Wilkinson
2. Client	Cracker Barrel Old Country Store (30th Anniversary)		7. Client	WaldenBooks/RIF Benefit
Designer	Paul Jarvis		Designer	Tyler Small

1.

2.

3.

4.

5.

6.

7.

8.

9.

10.

11.

12.

13.

14.

m●ses.com

m●ses.com

m●ses.com

15.

1 - 3, 5 - 8, 10 - 15
Design Firm Phoenix Creative
4, 9
Design Firm Cathey Associates, Inc.

1. Client	Anheuser-Busch/Aspen Ale	
Designer	Kathy Wilkinson	
2. Client	Kelty/Pangãea	
Designer	Kathy Wilkinson	
3. Client	Spectrum Brands	
Designer	Tyler Small	
4. Client	ahsum.com	
Designer	Matt Westapher	
5. Client	Think Tank/	
	Street Soccer Cup USA	
Designer	Steve Hicks	
6. Client	St. Louis Rams	
Designer	Kathy Wilkinson	
7. Client	Interventions for	
	Behavioral Change	
Designer	Steve Morris	

8. Client	Vie
Designer	Jenny Anderson
9. Client	Radcom Communications
	Integration
Designers	Matt Westapher
	& Gordon Cathey
10. Client	Washington University
	Visual Arts and Design Center
Designer	Deborah Finkelstein
11. Client	Borders/National Association
	of Recording Merchandisers
Designers	Deborah Finkelstein
	& Scott Ferguson
12. Client	Anne Ibur Creations
Designer	Deborah Finkelstein
13, 14	
Client	Maryville University of St. Louis
Designer	Ed Mantels-Seeker
15. Client	Moses.com
Designer	Elizabeth Williams

Freire *Charter School*

1.

R I N G I N G

Foundation **rocks**

2.

Arnosti
Consulting

3.

irre

**Institute for
Research and Reform
in Education**

4.

Global Crossing

5.

CARESIDE

6.

7.

1 - 4
Design Firm Joel Katz Design Associates
5 - 7
Design Firm Studio Morris

1. Client   Freire Charter School
    Designers   Mary Torrieri & Joel Katz

2. Client   Ringing Rocks Foundation
    Designers   Leslie Conner-Newbold
                      & Jennifer Long

3. Client   Arnosti Consulting
    Designer   Joel Katz

4. Client   Institute for Research
                      and Reform in Education
    Designers   Dave Schpok & Joel Katz

5. Client   Global Crossing
    Designer   Jeff Morris

6. Client   Careside
    Designer   Hyun Lee

7. Client   Coalition for The Homeless
    Designers   Jeff Morris & Kaoru Sato

(opposite)
Design Firm Lawson Design

    Client   Rubin Postaer & Assoc. for
                      American Century
    Designers   Jeff Lawson & Bob Francis

1.

2.

3.

4.

5.

6.

7.

8.

44

9.

The Printing Source Inc.

10.

NEWSLETTER FOR TECHNOLOGY GATEWAY

11.

12.

13.

14.

15.

1 - 8, 10 - 15
Design Firm AKA Design, Inc.

9

Design Firm Cathey Associates, Inc.

1.	Client	Commerce Magazine	8.	Client	YMCA of Greater St. Louis
	Designer	Stacy Lanier		Designer	John Ahearn
2.	Client	Baird, Kurtz & Dobson	9.	Client	Axxys Technologies
	Designers	Stacy Lanier & John Ahearn		Designer	Matt Westapher
3.	Client	St. Louis Hills Dental Group	10.	Client	The Printing Source
	Designers	Jim Jarvis & John Ahearn		Designer	Richie Murphy
4.	Client	Object Computing Inc.	11.	Client	Technology Gateway
	Designer	Mike Mullen		Designer	Virginia Schneider
5.	Client	Superior Waterproofing & Construction Related Restoration	12.	Client	Partners First
				Designer	Craig Martin Simon
	Designer	John Ahearn	13.	Client	Red Rock Studios
				Designer	Richie Murphy
6.	Client	Parkcrest Surgical Associates	14.	Client	AKA Design, Inc.
	Designer	Virginia Schneider		Designer	Richie Murphy
7.	Client	Splash City Waterpark	15.	Client	Energizer World
	Designers	Craig Martin Simon & Mike Mullen		Designer	Mike Mullen

1.

2.

3.

4.

5.

6.

BODYTONIC
HEALTH CLUB AND SPA

7.

8.

The Success Engine for Men and Women of Color

9.

Mountain Hound technologies

10.

Burke & ASSOCIATES

11.

NextWave
WIRELESS

12.

Microtech

13.

Trail Ridge Retirement Community

14.

15.

1 - 8, 10 - 15
Design Firm The Visual Group
9
Design Firm Cathey Associates, Inc.

1. Client	The Gorilla Search Group	
Designer	Ark Stein	
2. Client	Hewlett-Packard Company	
Designer	Ark Stein	
3. Client	Alchemedia, Inc.	
Designers	Lim Ng & Ark Stein	
4. Client	Alchemedia, Inc.	
Designers	Ark Stein & Lim Ng	
5. Client	NASA	
Designers	Lim Ng & Ark Stein	
6. Client	Supply-Line.com	
Designer	Lim Ng	
7. Client	Bodytonic	
Designer	Ark Stein	

8. Client	Beauty Clinica
Designer	Lim Ng
9. Client	ert1.com
Designer	Gordon Cathey
10. Client	Mountain Hound Technologies
Designer	Lim Ng
11. Client	Burke & Associates
Designer	Lim Ng
12. Client	NextWave Wireless
Designer	Lim Ng
13. Client	Microtech Systems
Designer	Ark Stein
14. Client	Trail Ridge
Designer	Lim Ng
15. Client	Jaffe Enterprises
Designer	Ark Stein

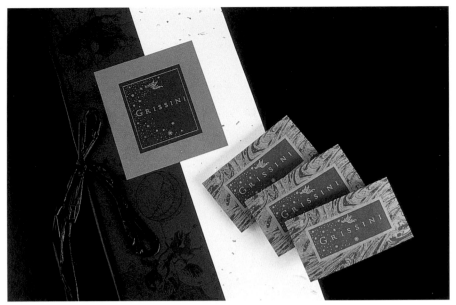

1.

2.

3.

4.

NIDUS™

5.

surfacine®

6.

7.

8.

conceptual capital

9.

10.

MITCHELL + HUGEBACK

1 - 3
Design Firm **Louey/Rubino Design Group, Inc.**

4 - 10
Design Firm **Phoenix Creative**

1. Client   Grissini
   Designer   Robert Louey

2. Client   Le Bar Bat
   Designer   Robert Louey

3. Client   Zen Palate
   Designer   Robert Louey

4. Client   Monsanto Company/
               Nidus Center
   Designer   Ed Mantels-Seeker

5. Client   Surfacine Development
               Company
   Designer   Ed Mantels-Seeker

6. Client   Places To Go
   Designer   Ed Mantels-Seeker

7. Client   Saint Louis Heroes/
               St. Louis 2004
   Designer   Ed Mantels-Seeker

8. Client   St. Louis Music/
               FlexWave Amplifiers
   Designers   Ed Mantels-Seeker
               & Luke Partridge

9. Client   Conceptual Capital
   Designer   Ed Mantels-Seeker

10. Client   Mitchell and Hugeback
               Architects
    Designer   Ed Mantels-Seeker

1.

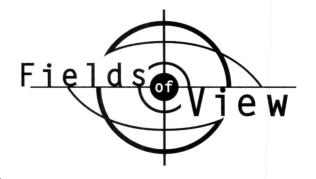

2.

3.

4.

5.

6.

7.

8.

Systems Consulting Group, Inc.

9.

STREETER

ASSOCIATES, INC.

10.

WELLSPRING

The Source for
Women's Health
and Fitness

11.

HOME
AND GARDEN
SHOW℠

12.

Living **Wise**

Choices *for*
Your Health

13.

14.

AVONLEA

FLORAL ARTS

15.

(all)

Design Firm Design Center

1. Client   Strategem
   Designers   John Reger
   Design Director:
                  Sherwin Schwartzrock

2. Client   Fields of View
   Designers   John Reger & Cory Dockew

3. Client   Taraccino Coffee
   Designers   John Reger & Todd Spichke

4. Client   Baileys Nursery
   Designers   John Reger
                  & Sherwin Schwartzrock

5. Client   Leef
   Designers   John Reger
                  & Sherwin Schwartzrock

6. Client   Noram
   Designers   John Reger
                  & Sherwin Schwartzrock

7. Client   Cameleon
   Designers   John Reger
                  & Sherwin Schwartzrock

8. Client   Oak Systems
   Designers   John Reger & Jon Erickson

9. Client   System Consulting Group
   Designers   John Reger, Sherwin
                  Schwartzrock & Jon Erickson

10. Client   Streeter & Associates
    Designers   John Reger
                   & Sherwin Schwartzrock

11. Client   Wellspring
    Designers   John Reger
                   & Sherwin Schwartzrock

12. Client   Home and Garden Show
    Designers   John Reger
                   & Sherwin Schwartztock

13. Client   Living Wise
    Designers   John Reger
                   & Sherwin Schwartzrock

14. Client   Resurrection Life Church
    Designers   John Reger
                   & Sherwin Schwartzrock

15. Client   Avonlea
    Designers   John Reger
                   & Sherwin Schwartzrock

Livestock™

1.

RIVERFRONT
CONCERTS

2.

SOLERA
REALTY & DEVELOPMENT

3.

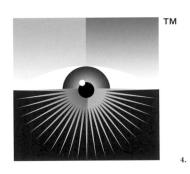

™

4.

AVANTIX
AVANTIX LABORATORIES, INC.

5.

VERITY™
INVESTIGATION AND RESPONSE

6.

RXVP

7.

1 - 7
Design Firm Orbit Integrated

1. Client   Livestock
    Designer   Jack Harris

2. Client   Delaware Theatre Company

3. Client   Solera Realty + Development
    Designer   Mark Miller

4. Client   New Media Insight
    Designer   Jack Harris

5. Client   Avantix Laboratories, Inc.
    Designer   Jack Harris

6. Client   Verity
    Designer   Jack Harris

7. Client   RXVP
    Designer   Jack Harris

(opposite)
Design Firm Squires & Company

    Client   Everlink
    Designer   Anna Magruder

EverLink™

Orbit.
integrated

1.

Animal Welfare Act

2.

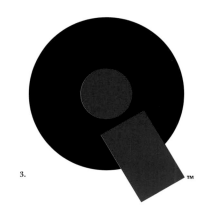

3.

4.

DELAWARE
THEATRE
COMPANY

5.

6.

7.

American Anti-Vivisection Society

8.

™

9.

10.

OF GREATER PHILADELPHIA

11.

12.

13.

14.

15.

1 - 11
Design Firm Orbit Integrated
12 - 14
Design Firm Phoenix Creative, St. Louis
15
Design Firm Studio Morris

1. Client	Orbit Integrated	
Designer	Jack Harris	
2. Client	American Anti-Vivisection Society	
Designer	Jack Harris	
3. Client	Orbit Integrated	
Designer	Jack Harris	
4. Client	ABHA	
Designer	Jack Harris	
5. Client	Delaware Theatre Company	
Designer	Jack Harris	
6. Client	DC Comics	
Designer	Jack Harris	
7. Client	American Anti-Vivisection Society	
Designer	Jack Harris	

8. Client	American Anti-Vivisection Society	
Designer	Jack Harris	
9. Client	Environmental Alliance	
Designer	Jack Harris	
10. Client	Visual Logic	
Designer	Jack Harris	
11. Client	Lawyer Connection of Gr. Philadelphia	
Designer	Jack Harris	
12. Client	Anheuser-Busch National Retail Sales	
Designer	Ed Mantels-Seeker	
13. Client	Murder City Players	
Designer	Ed Mantels-Seeker	
14. Client	Big Brothers Big Sisters of Greater St. Louis	
Designer	Deborh Finkelstein	
15. Client	Homespace	
Designer	Hyun Lee	

55

1.

3.

CALIFORNIA

4.

5.

6.

BRANDYE
JAMES
DIRECTOR

7.

8.

9.

10.

11.

12.

VENTURE CAPITAL FORUM
FOR HIGH GROWTH & TECHNOLOGY COMPANIES

13.

14.

15.

1 - 6
Design Firm Funk and Associates
7 - 8
Design Firm Squires & Company
9 - 15
Design Firm AKA Design, Inc.

1. Client	Eugene Public Library Foundation	
Designers	Beverly Soasey & Kathleen Heinz	
2. Client	Dan Tucci	
Designers	Beverly Soasey & Christopher Berner	
3. Client	City of Clovis, CA	
Designer	Christopher Berner	
4. Client	States Industries	
Designer	Christopher Berner	
5. Client	CBSI (Revenue Maximization)	
Designer	Krista Lippert	
6. Client	CBSI (DVT)	
Designer	Krista Lippert	
7. Client	Brandye James	
Designer	Paul Black	

8. Client	Balboa
Designer	Paul Black
9. Client	Credo
Designers	John Ahearn & Sara Gries
10. Client	Collegiate Entrepreneur of the Year
Designers	Richie Murphy & John Ahearn
11. Client	Graduate School, USDA
Designer	Mike Mullen
12. Client	Energizer
Designer	Richie Murphy
13. Client	Invest Midwest
Designer	Richie Murphy
14. Client	Eastport Business Center
Designers	Virginia Schneider & John Ahearn
15. Client	Recreation Station
Designers	Stacy Lanier & Craig Martin Simon

1.

2.

3.

4.

5.

6.

7.

(opposite)
Design Firm Dixon & Parcels Associates, Inc.

Client   Eggland's Best, Inc.

1 - 7
Design Firm AKA Design, Inc.

1. Client   Grant's Farm
   Designer Mike Mullen

2. Client   Southwestern Illinois
             Tourism Bureau
   Designer Craig Martin Simon

3. Client   No Sox Charity Ball Team
   Designer Richie Murphy

4. Client   Kehrs Mill Dental
   Designers Richie Murphy & John Ahearn

5. Client   Kirkwood/Webster YMCA
   Designer John Ahearn

6. Client   Infinitech
   Designer John Ahearn

7. Client   St. Louis Regional Chamber
             & Growth Association
   Designers Richie Murphy & John Ahearn

BANK OF PETALUMA

1.

TamalpaisBank

2.

kitcole™
investment advisory services

3.

4.

myplay

5.

6.

handspring

7.

springboard

8.

9.

Children's Council of San Francisco

10.

CALIFORNIA

11.

12.

SAFER
SAN FRANCISCO
EARTHQUAKE
RETROFIT

13.

14.

15.

1 - 8
Design Firm Mortensen Design
9 - 15
Design Firm The Visual Group

1. Client   Bank of Petaluma
   Designers Gordon Mortensen,
              Wendy Chon, & Chris Gall

2. Client   Tamalpais Bank
   Designers Wendy Chon
              & Gordon Mortensen

3. Client   Kit Cole Investment
              Advisory Services
   Designers Gordon Mortensen
              & Wendy Chon

4. Client   Eazel
   Designers PJ Nidecker
              & Gordon Mortensen

5. Client   MyPlay, Inc.
   Designers PJ Nidecker
              & Gordon Mortensen

6. Client   CallTheShots
   Designers Gordon Mortensen
              & Wendy Chon

7. Client   Handspring
   Designers PJ Nidecker
              & Gordon Mortensen

8. Client   Handspring, Inc.
   Designers PJ Nidecker
              & Gordon Mortensen

9. Client   Peninsula Community
              Foundation
   Designers Lim Ng & Ark Stein

10. Client   Children Council
              of San Francisco
    Designer Ark Stein

11. Client   Peninsula Foods
    Designer Ark Stein

12. Client   Uncle Luigi Pizza
    Designer Ark Stein

13. Client   Caltrans
    Designer Ark Stein

14. Client   Izzy's Brooklyn Bagels
    Designers Bill Mifsud & Ark Stein

15. Client   USC
    Designer Ark Stein

1.

2.

NORTHSTAR

3.

SetRite™

4.

5.

IZZY'S
BROOKLYN
BAGELS

6.

7.

(all)
Design Firm CUBE Advertising & Design

1. Client   Life Uniform
   Designer   David Chiow

2. Client   Life Uniform
   Designer   David Chiow

3. Client   Northstar Management Co.
   Designers   David Chiow & Matt Marino

4. Client   Crown Theraputics, Inc.
   Designer   David Chiow

5. Client   Anheuser-Busch, Inc.
   Designers   David Chiow & Kevin Hough

6. Client   The Natural Way
   Designer   David Chiow

7. Client   dreyfus + associates photography
   Designer   David Chiow

(opposite)
Design Firm CUBE Advertising & Design

   Client   St. Louis Zoo
   Designer   David Chiow

TRANSCORE

1.

2.

SPRINGHILL
SUITES™
Marriott.

3.

EXECUSTAY
CORPORATE HOUSING SOLUTIONS
Marriott®

4.

EPICYTE
PHARMACEUTICAL INC.

5.

Family
SERVICES

6.

S·P·I·R·I·T

7.

8.

M I R A P O I N T

9.

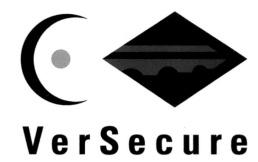

VerSecure

10.

Junglee

11.

PALM
COMPUTING
PLATFORM

12.

HORICON
STATE BANK

13.

$\mathcal{G}$

GROWTH
N E T W O R K S

14.

PANTERA INTERNATIONAL

15.

1 - 8		
Design Firm	**Bailey Design Group, Inc.**	
9 - 14		
Design Firm	**Mortensen Design**	
15		
Design Firm	**Theodore C. Alexander, Jr.**	

1.	Client	Transcore
	Designer	Laura Markley
2.	Client	Bailey Design Group, Inc.
	Designer	Gary LaCroix
3.	Client	Marriott Corporation
	Designers	Wendy Slavish & Steve Perry
4.	Client	Marriott Corporation
	Designer	David Fiedler
5.	Client	Epicyte Pharmaceutical
	Designer	Steve Perry
6.	Client	Family Services
	Designer	Steve Perry
7.	Client	Spirit
	Designer	David Fiedler

8.	Client	Annabelle Properties
	Designer	Steve Perry
9.	Client	Mirapoint, Inc.
	Designers	PJ Nidecker
		& Gordon Mortensen
10.	Client	Hewlett-Packard
	Designers	Diana Kauzlarich
		& Gordon Mortensen
11.	Client	Junglee Corporation
	Designers	Diana Kauzlarich
		& Gordon Mortensen
12.	Client	Palm Computing
	Designers	Gordon Mortensen
		& Wendy Chon
13.	Client	Horicon Bank
	Designers	Wendy Chon
		& Gordon Mortensen
14.	Client	Growth Networks
	Designers	Wendy Chon
		& Gordon Mortensen
15.	Client	Pantera International
	Designer	Theodore C. Alexander

1.

2.

3.

4.

The Smittcamp Family
HONORS COLLEGE
California State University, Fresno

5.

6.

7.

8.

Paul E. Lerandeau
ATTORNEY AT LAW

9.

10.

11.

THE
KEN ROBERTS
Gallery

12.

GROWING NEW VENTURES

13.

14.

15.

(all)

Design Firm Shields Design

1.	Client Designers	Attitude Online Juan Vega & Charles Shields	8.	Client Designers	The Zone Sportsplex Charles Shields & Stephanie Wong
2.	Client Designers	Valley Children's Hospital Laura Thornton & Charles Shields	9.	Client Designers	Paul E. Lerandeau Thoms Kimmelman & Charles Shields
3.	Client Designers	Digital Production Group Thomas Kimmelman & Charles Shields	10.	Client Designer	Baker, Manock & Jensen Charles Shields
4.	Client Designers	Heberger & Company Charles Shields & Stephanie Wong	11.	Client Designer	Phil Rudy Photography Charles Shields
5.	Client Designers	Smittcamp Family Honors College Charles Shields & Stephanie Wong	12.	Client Designer	The Ken Roberts Company Charles Shields
6.	Client Designer	The Ken Roberts Company Charles Shields	13.	Client Designer	Central Valley Business Incubator Charles Shields
7.	Client Designer	Great Pacific Trading Company Charles Shields	14.	Client Designer	The Ken Roberts Company Charles Shields
			15.	Client Designer	The Ken Roberts Company Charles Shields

1.

2.

3.

4.

5.

6.

7.

(opposite)
Design Firm **McElveney & Palozzi**
Design Group, Inc.

Client   Mayer Bros.
Designers   William McElveney
                & Lisa Parenti

1 - 7
Design Firm **McElveney & Palozzi**
Design Group, Inc.

1. Client   Fowler Farms
    Designers   William McElveney, Matt
                Nowicki, & Jan Marie Gallagher

2. Client   Atwater Foods Inc.
    Designers   Bill McElveney
                & Lisa Williamson

3. Client   The Lodge at Woodcliff
    Designers   William McElveney
                & Ellen Johnson

4. Client   The Lodge at Woodcliff
    Designers   William McElveney
                & Ellen Johnson

5. Client   LeRoy Village Green
    Designers   William McElveney, Lisa Parenti,
                & Jan Marie Gallagher

6. Client   Fieldbrook Farms Inc.
    Designers   William McElveney
                & Ellen Johnson

7. Client   Spring Street Society
    Designer   Steve Palozzi

THE ELLIOTT

1.

palouse

2.

Starting Early
STARTING SMART

3.

ESM CONSULTING ENGINEERS

4.

redley

5.

iridio

6.

FRYE
ART MUSEUM

7.

ARTIST TRUST
IT BEGINS WITH THE ARTIST

8.

70

NEWHOLLY

9.

HENRY M. JACKSON
FOUNDATION

10.

PC Assistance
INCORPORATED

11.

MATERIAL CONTROL
RX

12.

Walter Dyer's
SHOES & LEATHER

13.

Alliance™
BY FACTURA

14.

DESIGN GROUP INC.

15.

1 - 10				
Design Firm	**The Traver Company**		8. Client	The Artist Trust Fund
11 - 15			Designer	David Cox
Design Firm	**McElveney & Palozzi**			
	Design Group		9. Client	Popkin Development
			Designer	Christopher Downs
1. Client	RC Hedreen Co.			
Designers	Dale Hart		10. Client	Henry M. Jackson Foundation
	& Christopher Downs		Designer	Margo Sepanski
2. Client	Palouse		11. Client	PC Assistance Inc.
Designer	Christopher Downs		Designers	William McElveney
				& Lisa Williamson
3. Client	The Casey Family Program			
Designer	Christopher Downs		12. Client	Auto-Soft
			Designers	Jon Westfall & Steve Palozzi
4. Client	ESM Consulting Engineers			
Designers	Dale Hart & Christopher Downs		13. Client	Walter Dyer's Shoes & Leather
			Designers	Matt Nowicki & Paul Reisinger
5. Client	Redley			
Designer	Dale Hart		14. Client	Factura
			Designers	Steve Palozzi & Matt Nowicki
6. Client	Iridio			
Designers	Christopher Downs,		15. Client	McElveney & Palozzi
	Margo Sepanski, Dale Hart,			Design Group
	& Hugh Rodman		Designers	Jon Westfall, William McElveney,
				& Steve Palozzi
7. Client	Frye Art Museum			
Designer	Margo Sepanski			

The
Council of
Faiths

1.

NEW CANAAN
COMMUNITY
FOUNDATION

2.

3.

4.

5.

6.

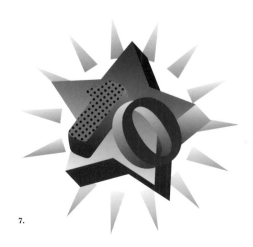

7.

8.

9.

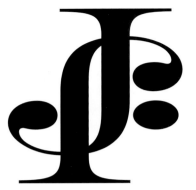

10.

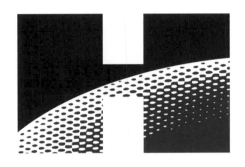

11.

12.

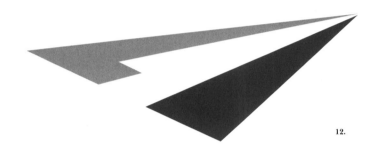

13.

14.

15.

1 - 13			7. Client	BMG
Design Firm	**Congdon & Company LLC**		Designer	Arthur Congdon
14 - 15				
Design Firm	**McElveney & Palozzi Design Group**		8. Client	Delaware Valley Distributing
			Designer	Arthur Congdon
1. Client	Council of Faiths of Southwestern Connecticut		9. Client	Mercury Marine
Designer	Arthur Congdon		Designer	Arthur Congdon
2. Client	New Canaan Connecticut Community Foundation		10. Client	Jeniam Foundation
Designer	Arthur Congdon		Designer	Athur Congdon
3. Client	New Canaan (Connecticut) High School Madrigal Ensemble		11. Client	Hypernex
Designer	Arthur Congdon		Designer	Arthur Congdon
4. Client	New Canaan (Connecticut) High School Madrigal Ensemble		12. Client	Corp Air
Designer	Arthur Congdon		Designer	Arthur Congdon
5. Client	Biosense Webster, Johnson & Johnson Co.		13. Client	Ortho-McNeil
Designer	Arthur Congdon		Designer	Arthur Congdon
6. Client	Novasource		14. Client	G-Force Collaborations
Designer	Arthur Congdon		Designers	William McElveney, Matt Nowicki, & Dillon Constable
			15. Client	Abbott's Frozen Custard
			Designers	Bill McElveney & Lisa Parenti

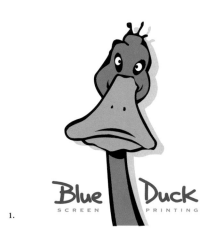

1.

2.

3.

4.

5.

6.

7.

8.

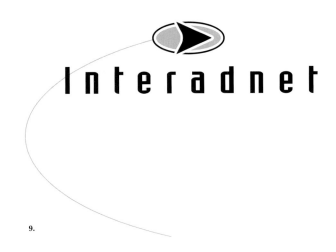

Interadnet

9.

FROG EXPRESS

10.

GLOBE

11.

T  P

12.

13.

ST. PATRICK
PARTNERSHIP CENTER

14.

15.

(all)
Design Firm Bartels & Company, Inc.

1. Client   Blue Duck Screen Printing
   Designers   David Bartels
                 & Ron Rodemacher

2. Client   Blue Deep, Ltd.
   Designers   David Bartels, Mary Flock,
                 & Chris Schott

3. Client   UI

4. Client   Testrip
   Designers   David Bartels
                 & Ron Rodemacher

5. Client   Executive Expression
   Designers   Ron Rodemacher
                 & David Bartels

6. Client   American Manicure
   Designers   Ron Rodemacher, David Bartels,
                 & Don Strander

7. Client   Sacred Heart Villa
   Designer   Bob Thomas

8. Client   Micell Technologies, Inc.
   Designers   Ron Rodemacher
                 & David Bartels

9. Client   Interadnet
   Designers   Chris Schott & David Bartels

10. Client   Frog Express
    Designers   David Bartels &
                 Ron Rodemacher

11. Client   The Sandcastle
    Designers   Ron Rodemacher &
                 David Bartels

12. Client   Top Graphics
    Designers   Ron Rodemacher &
                 David Bartels

13. Client   Generalife Insurance Company
    Designers   David Bartels &
                 Ron Rodemacher

14. Client   St. Patrick Partnership Center
    Designers   Ron Rodemacher &
                 David Bartels

15. Client   Ceci Bartels Associates
    Designer   Ron Rodemacher

1.

WASHINGTON AREA

LAWYERS FOR THE ARTS

2.

3.

MV/S

4.

WiNK

5.

6.

AERIE

networks

7.

all kinds of minds

A NON-PROFIT INSTITUTE FOR THE
UNDERSTANDING OF DIFFERENCES IN LEARNING   8.

BUTTERFLY WING
SAINT LOUIS ZOO

9.

10.

11.

12.

SpectrAlliance

13.

Therapoint™

14.

15.

1 - 4
Design Firm Axis Communications
5 - 8
Design Firm Doublespace
9 - 15
Design Firm CUBE Advertising & Design

1. Client   Merchandising East
    Designers   Charlyne Fabi & Craig Byers

2. Client   Washington Area Lawyers
                  for the Arts
    Designers   Chris Walker & Craig Byers

3. Client   Sitta Fine Art
    Designers   Tamara Dowd & Craig Byers

4. Client   Michael V. Statham
    Designers   Charlyne Fabi & Craig Byers

5. Client   Wink
    Designers   Jane Kosstrin & Jason Endres

6. Client   Visualcities
    Designers   Evelyn Bernhard
                  & Jane Kosstrin

7. Client   Aerie Networks
    Designers   Jane Kosstrin & Sally Slavens

8. Client   All Kinds of Minds
    Designers   Jane Kosstrin & Jesse Woodward

9. Client   Saint Louis Zoo
    Designers   David Chiow & Kevin Hough

10. Client   David Kingsbury Photography
    Designer   David Chiow

11. Client   Anheuser-Busch, Inc.
    Designers   David Chiow & Kevin Hough

12. Client   Clayco Construction Company
    Designers   David Chiow & Kevin Hough

13. Client   SpectrAlliance, Inc.
    Designers   David Chiow & Kevin Hough

14. Client   Crown Therapeutics, Inc.
    Designer   David Chiow

15. Client   Anheuser-Busch, Inc.
    Designers   David Chiow & Kevin Hough

Market Central™

1.

2.

SERRANO HOTEL
SAN FRANCISCO

3.

4.

5.

DENNY
EYE & LASER
CENTER

6.

7.

(opposite)
Design Firm Bailey Design Group, Inc.

Client   Compass Group of America

3 -4
Design Firm McGaughy Design
5 -9
Design Firm Hunt Weber Clark
             Associates, Inc.

1. Client   National Postal Forum
    Designer Malcolm McGaughy

2. Client   McGaughy Design
    Designer Malcolm McGaughy

3. Client   Kimpton Hotel
              & Restaurant Group
    Designers Jim Deeken
              & Nancy Hunt-Weber

4. Client   Joie deVivre Hospitality
    Designers Nancy Hunt-Weber
              & Christine Chung

5. Client   Hawthorne Lane
    Designers Nancy Hunt-Weber & Jason Bell

6. Client   Denny Eye + Laser Center
    Designers Christine Chung
              & Nancy Hunt-Weber

7. Client   epropose
    Designers Jason Bell & Nancy Hunt-Weber

1.

2.

3.

4.

BUSINESS GROUPS

5.

6.

7.

8.

9.

10.

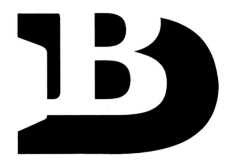

11.

12.

13.

14.

15.

LifeSongs
GIVING VOICE TO THE SPIRIT WITHIN

1.

Fresh Air
2.

sensations
a w a k e n
to
the Richness of Life

scent

how often we associate the warmth
of a place or event with the memory
of a scent. scent is nostalgia's best
friend. the impression of smell lingers
in us longer and evokes reflection
more than any other sense.

3.

Gardens
a n d
MEMORIES

4.

Portfolio
BY HALLMARK

5.

Symbolic Notions

6.

7.

1 - 7
Design Firm Hallmark Cards, Inc.

1. Client   Hallmark Cards
    Designer   Peg Carlson-Hoffman

2. Client   Hallmark Cards
    Designer   Peg Carlson-Hoffman

3. Client   Hallmark Cards
    Designer   Sean Branagan

4. Client   Hallmark Cards
    Designer   Barb Mizik

5. Client   Hallmark Cards
    Designer   John Marak

6. Client   Hallmark Cards
    Designer   Erica Becker

7. Client   Hallmark Cards
    Designer   Jake Mikolic

(opposite)
Design Firm Bailey Design Group, Inc.

    Client   Cultivations
    Designers   Tisha Armour, David Fiedler,
                  & Christian Williamson

82

ALL MALT
VIENNA STYLE LAGER

1.

KÖLSCH STYLE
SUMMER MALT ALE

2.

3.

4.

5.

6.

7.

8.

9.

10.

11.

12.

13.

14.

15.

(all)
Design Firm Compass Design

1 - 3
  Client   August Schell Brewing Co.
  Designers Mitchell Lindgren, Tom Arthur,
              & Rich McGowen

4 - 7
  Client   Buckin' Bass Brewing Co.
  Designers Mitchell Lindgren, Tom Arthur,
              & Rich McGowen

8 - 10
  Client   Great Waters Brewing Co.
  Designers Mitchell Lindgren, Tom Arthur,
              & Rich McGowen

11 - 15
  Client   World Wide Sports
  Designers Mitchell Lindgren, Tom Arthur,
              & Rich McGowen

1.

2.

3.

4.

5.

6.

7.

8.

9.

10.

11.

12.

13.

14.

15.

1 - 6
Design Firm L.J. Sands & Associates
7 - 10
Design Firm Bruce Yelaska Design
11 - 15
Design Firm Wet Paper Bag Graphic Design

1.	Client	Aacres Allvest	8. Client	Messenger Cards
	Designer	Mary Pugliese	Designer	Bruce Yelaska
2.	Client	Harbor Air		
	Designer	Courtenay Watson	9. Client	The Gauntlett Group
			Designer	Bruce Yelaska
3.	Client	Commencement Terrace		
	Designer	Mary Pugliese	10. Client	Simmons, Ungar, Helbush, Steinberg & Bright
4.	Client	Outlook	Designer	Bruce Yelaska
	Designer	Mary Pugliese		
5.	Client	Primo Grill	11. Client	Laser Impact
	Designer	Mary Pugliese	Designer	Lewis Glaser
6.	Client	St. Andrews	12. Client	Geocities Inc.
	Designer	Mary Pugliese	Designer	Lewis Glaser
7.	Client	Millennium Restaurant Consultants	13. Client	TCU Student Development Services
			Designer	Lewis Glaser
	Designer	Bruce Yelaska	14. Client	J & D Productions
			Designer	Lewis Glaser
			15. Client	Texas Christian University Graphic Design Program
			Designer	Lewis Glaser

1.

The Internet Performance Authority

2.

LADYLIKE
PRODUCTIONS

3.

4.

5.

CertifiedTime.com

6.

7.

überbabe™ media, inc.

(opposite)
Design Firm	**Bruce Yelaska Design**	
Client	Hunan Garden	
Designer	Bruce Yelaska	

1 - 7
Design Firm Coda Creative, Inc.

1. Client — Keynote Systems
   Designers — Paola Coda & Kurt Stammberger

2. Client — Ladylike Productions
   Designers — Pavida Hoparsatsuk & Kurt Stammberger

3. Client — Splash Studios
   Designers — Mark Deamer & Paola Coda

4. Client — RSA Data Security Conference 1999
   Designers — Paola Coda & Kurt Stammberger

5. Client — Certified Time
   Designers — Paola Coda & Kurt Stammberger

6. Client — RSA Data Security
   Designers — Paola Coda & Kurt Stammberger

7. Client — überbabe media, inc.
   Designers — Lisa Voldeng & Ashley Phelps

1.

2.

CARPE DATUM

5.

Fleur de Lis
COMMUNICATIONS

4.

7.

FIELD OF DREAMS
enterprises

6.

ROCKY COASTS

SENECA PARK ZOO

8.

9.

10.

11.

12.

13.

Goody Goody Gumdrops

14.

15.

1.

2.

DREAM WIZARDS

3.

PAPILIO

4.

5.

SANS SOUCI PRESS

6.

7.

1 - 7

Design Firm Designsmith

1. Client   Teachers Affect Eternity/
               The Education People
   Designer   Richard Smith

2. Client   Celebrate Learning/
               The Education People
   Designer   Richard Smith

3. Client   Dream Wizards
   Designer   Richard Smith

4. Client   Papilio
   Designer   Richard Smith

5. Client   The Future Begins/
               The Education People
   Designer   Richard Smith

6. Client   Sans Souci Press
   Designer   Richard Smith

7. Client   Kids First/
               The Education People
   Designer   Richard Smith

(opposite)
Design Firm Bailey Design Group, Inc.

   Client   Compass Group of America
   Designer   Steve Perry

on display

1.

KATSIN/LOEB

creative jocks

2.

big Score   big Score   big Score

3.

BOOST WORKS

4.

friends of ocean beach

5.

6.

TELL·GET

LOYALTY
LOOP

KEEP·BUILD

7.

BUSINESS
AFTER HOURS

8.

9.

10.

11.

SPECIALTY DESIGN STUDIO

12.

13.

studio B

14.

15.

1 - 2
Design Firm Rubber Design
3 - 5
Design Firm Duncan/Channon
6 - 7
Design Firm Griffith Phillips Creative
8
Design Firm double entendre
9 - 15
Design Firm Hallmark Cards, Inc.

1. Client   Stoneridge Shopping Center
    Designer   Jacquie VanKeuren

2. Client   Katsin-Loeb Advertising
    Designer   Jacquie VanKeuren

3. Client   Big Score
    Designer   Jacquie VanKeuren

4. Client   Boostworks
    Designer   Jacquie VanKeuren

5. Client   California Coastal Commission
    Designer   Jacquie VanKeuren

6. Client   Craig Varjabedian Photography
    Designer   Alan Benest

7. Client   GPCInteractive -
                  Loyalty Loop Program
    Designer   Brian Niemann

8. Client   Greater Seattle
                  Chamber of Commerce
    Designers   Daniel P. Smith
                  & Richard A. Smith

9. Client   Hallmark Cards
    Designer   Jake Mikolic

10. Client   Specialty Design
    Designer   Jake Mikolic

11. Client   Hallmark Cards
    Designer   Sean Branagan

12. Client   Specialty Design
    Designer   Barb Mizik

13. Client   Specialty Design
    Designer   Jake Mikolic

14. Client   Specialty Design
    Designer   Jake Mikolic

15. Client   Specialty Design
    Designer   Lee Stork

1.

PACIFIC
ECHO

2.

Committed to
Excellence

3.

·ROR·

4.

BURKE WILLIAMS

5.

 ZINERA

6.

ZIG ZIGLAR NETWORK

7.

THE
METROPOLITAN
OPERA

8.

CLASSIC

LANDSCAPE

9.

ANDERSON

FUNERAL HOME, LTD.

10.

SASAir, Inc.

11.

DESIGN

12.

school of

THEATRE & DANCE

13.

NEW DESTINY

FILMS

14.

15.

1 - 3		
Design Firm	**Designsmith**	
4 - 7		
Design Firm	**Shimokochi/Reeves**	
8		
Design Firm	**World Studio**	
9 - 13		
Design Firm	**B² Design**	
14 - 15		
Design Firm	**Dotzler Creative Arts**	

1.	Client	The Flying Cork Club/ Pacific Echo Cellars
	Designer	Richard Smith
2.	Client	Pacific Echo
	Designer	Richard Smith
3.	Client	Committed to Excellence/ The Education People
	Designer	Richard Smith
4.	Client	ROR
	Designers	Mamoru Shimokochi, Anne Reeves, & Eugene Bustillos
5.	Client	Burke Williams
	Designers	Mamoru Shimokochi & Anne Reeves
6.	Client	Zig Ziglar Network
	Designers	Mamoru Shimokochi & Anne Reeves

7.	Client	Zig Ziglar Network
	Designers	Mamory Shimokochi & Anne Reeves
8.	Client	The Metropolitan Opera
	Designers	David Sterling, Mark Randall, Jeroen Jas, Stefan Hengst, Klaus Kempenaars & Michael Samuels
9.	Client	Classic Landscape
	Designer	Carol M. Benthal-Bingley
10.	Client	Anderson Funeral Home
	Designers	Julie Wojak & Carol Benthal-Bingley
11.	Client	SASAir, Inc.
	Designer	Carol M. Benthal-Bingley
12.	Client	B² Design
	Designer	Carol Benthal-Bingley
13.	Client	Northern Illinois University School of Theatre and Dance
	Designer	Carol Benthal-Bingley
14.	Client	New Destiny Films
15.	Client	Trinity Church

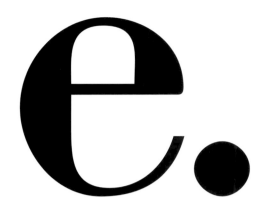

1.

DIVI RESTAURANT

2.

3.

4.

314 434 7237

5.

HARMONY™

6.

 LABARGE CLAYCO WIRELESS, LLC

7.

SSMA℠

(opposite)
Design Firm E. Tajima Creative Group, Inc.

Client   E. Tajima Creative Group, Inc.
Designers   Roz Roos Designs for the
                   E. Tajima Creative Group, Inc.

1 - 8
Design Firm CUBE Advertising & Design
9
Design Firm J G M Design

1. Client   Divi Restaurant
    Designer   David Chiow

2. Client   Clayco Construction Company
    Designers   David Chiow & Kevin Hough

3. Client   Saint Louis Zoo
    Designer   David Chiow

4. Client   Retail Results
    Designer   David Chiow

5. Client   Crown Therapeutics, Inc.
    Designer   David Chiow

6. Client   LaBarge Clayco Wireless, LLC
    Designers   Steve Wienke & David Chiow

7. Client   Steel Stud Manufacturers
                     Association
    Designer   Joan Gilbert Madsen

1.

2.

3.

4.

5.

6.

7.

8.

9.

10.

11.

12.

13.

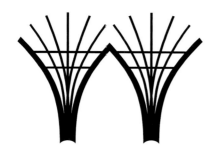

14.

15.

1 - 9
Design Firm Hess Design Inc.
10 - 15
**Design Firm Michael Lee Advertising
& Design, Inc.**

1. Client   Invisuals
    Designer   Karyn Goba

2. Client   Strategix Solutions
    Designer   Karyn Goba

3. Client   CELT Corp.
    Designer   Kim Daly

4. Client   Equity Industrial Partners
    Designer   Kim Daly

5. Client   Perfect Form
    Designer   Kim Daly

6. Client   Ristino Strategic
                 Communications
    Designer   Jim Harrington

7. Client   the Baker Group
    Designers   Kim Daly & Karyn Goba

8. Client   Trippics.Com
    Designers   Kim Daly & Melissa Meinhold

9. Client   The Clean Machine
    Designers   Hannah Gilmore
                 & Heather Knopf

10. Client   SOLD4U
    Designer   Michael Lee

11. Client   EMSfile
    Designer   Michael Lee

12. Client   TelDataComm
    Designer   Michael Lee

13. Client   Wester Landscape Management
    Designer   Michael Lee

14. Client   Efficient Systems
    Designer   Michael Lee

15. Client   On Stage Hair Design
    Designer   Michael Lee

1.

EL'E MEN TAL'

2.

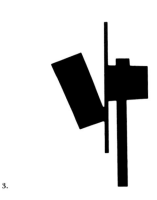

3.

Loyalty Leads the Way

4.

Presbytery of Philadelphia

5.

Oryx

6.

7.

1 - 3
Design Firm EAI
4 - 6
Design Firm Art 270, Inc.
7
Design Firm Schlatter Design

1. Client   The Coca-Cola Company
   Designer Todd Simmons

2. Client   Elemental Interactive Design
               & Development
   Designer Matt Rollins

3. Client   Human Arts Gallery
   Designer Matt Rollins

4. Client   Beaver College
   Designer John Opet

5. Client   Presbytery of Philadelphia
   Designers Carl Mill, Sean Flanagan,
               & Holly Kempf

6. Client   LHS Priority Call
   Designer Holly Kempf

7. Client   Green Thumb Organics, Inc.
   Designer Richard Schlatter

(opposite)
Design Firm Bailey Design Group, Inc.

Client   Marriott Corporation
Designer David Fiedler

EXECUTIVE RESIDENCES℠

1.

2.

RESOURCE

3.

CATHOLIC

SOCIAL

SERVICES

OF SOUTHWESTERN OHIO

4.

POLO·GRILLE

5.

CRICKETS

AFTER HOURS

6.

Apptitude™

7.

CLOSET ™
DIMENSIONS

8.

104

9.

JOHNFRANK

10.

11.

MICHAEL GRAVES
DESIGN™

12.

THEATER ZERO

13.

ORGANIC CLOVER COTTON

14.

thirteen hour sale

15.

13

<table>
1 - 6				
Design Firm	**Five Visual Communication & Design**		8. Client	Closet Dimensions
			Designer	Jennifer Sonderby
7 - 10				
Design Firm	**Lux Design**		9. Client	allCharities.com
11 - 15			Designer	Laura Cary
Design Firm	**Design Guys**			
			10. Client	John Frank
1. Client	Pasta Basket		Designer	Jennifer Sonderby
Designer	Rondi Tschopp			
			11. Client	Target Stores
2. Client	Designing Women		Designers	Amy Kirkpatrick &
Designers	Rondi Tschopp & Denry Fagan			Anne Peterson
			Lettering	Todd ap Jones
3. Client	Resource1		12. Client	Target Stores
Designers	Denry Fagan & Rondi Tschopp		Designer	Scott Thares
4. Client	Catholic Social Services		13. Client	Theater Zero
Designer	Rondi Tschopp		Designer	Joseph Kral
5. Client	Polo Grille		14. Client	Target Stores
Designers	Denmy Fagan & Rondi Tschopp		Designer	Jay Theige
6. Client	Crickets		15. Client	Dayton, Hudson, Marshall Field's
Designers	Denny Fagan & Rondi Tschopp			
7. Client	Apptitude		Designer	Jay Theige
Designer	Jennifer Sonderby			
</table>

1.

A Spa for Hands and Feet

2.

3.

4.

5.

6.

7.

8.

106

9.

10.

11.

12.

13.

14.

SYMPLECTIC
ENGINEERING CORPORATION

15.

1 - 8					
Design Firm	**Vrontikis Design Office**		8.	Client	WEA-Warner/Elektra/Atlantic
9 - 15				Designers	David Schweiger
Design Firm	**Linden Design/LogoGuy**				& Petrula Vrontikis
1.	Client	Global-Dining, Inc.	9.	Client	Harold Hedelman
	Designers	Tammy Kim & Petrula Vrontikis		Designer	Stephen Linden
2.	Client	Hands On Day Spas	10.	Client	Scientific Learning
	Designers	Peggy Woo & Petrula Vrontikis		Designer	Stephen Linden
3.	Client	William Jackson/Cybergourmet	11.	Client	CFI
	Designer	Petrula Vrontikis		Designer	Stephen Linden
4.	Client	Global Music One	12.	Client	Scientific Learning
	Designers	Marilyn Prado		Designer	Stephen Linden
		& Petrula Vrontikis	13.	Client	GeoVector
5.	Client	Global Music One		Designer	Stephen Linden
	Designers	Laura Leiman	14.	Client	Symplectic Engineering
		& Petrula Vrontikis		Designer	Stephen Linden
6.	Client	Steve Ross/Maha Yoga	15.	Client	Celestial Mechanics
	Designer	Petrula Vrontikis		Designer	Stephen Linden
7.	Client	Warner/Elektra/Atlantic-WEA			
	Designers	Peggy Woo & Petrula Vrontikis			

1.

VILLAGE

JOINERY

2.

Slinging Star

3.

4.

5.

6.

The Remote Access Software Solution!

7.

kindercotton.com

(opposite)
Design Firm Bailey Design Group, Inc.

Client   Marriott Corporation
Designer   Gary LaCroix

1 - 7
Design Firm Stratford Design Associates

1. Client   Village Joinery
    Designer   Silvia Stephenson

2. Client   Slinging Star
    Designer   Tim Gerould

3. Client   ICF
    Designer   Silvia Stephenson

4. Client   SUS
    Designer   Tim Gerould

5. Client   Beals Martin
    Designers   Gerald Stratford, Sr.
                & Tim Gerould

6. Client   Cisco
    Designers   Gerald Stratford, Sr.
                & Rebecca Lambing

7. Client   Kindercotton
    Designer   Silvia Stephenson

1.

interactive edge

2.

>>ezitem

GEMINI

3.

A R I E S

4.

HEARTSEASE HOME

5.

6.

7.

8.

110

9.

10.

11.

12.

13.

14.

nSite Software, Inc.

15.

1.

2.

3.

4.

5.

6.

7.

1 - 7

Design Firm **Compass Design**

1. Client   Nikola's Biscotti
   Designers   Mitchell Lindgren, Tom Arthur,
                     & Rich McGowen

2. Client   Juntunen Media Group
   Designers   Mitchell Lindgren, Tom Arthur,
                     & Rich McGowen

3. Client   Lars Hansen Photography
   Designers   Mitchell Lindgren, Tom Arthur,
                     & Rich McGowen

4. Client   Metropolitan Hodder Group
   Designers   Mitchell Lindgren, Tom Arthur,
                     & Rich McGowen

5. Client   World Wide Sports
   Designers   Mitchell Lindgren, Tom Arthur,
                     & Rich McGowen

6. Client   International Foods, Inc.
   Designers   Mitchell Lindgren, Tom Arthur,
                     & Rich McGowen

7. Client   Red Wing Foods
   Designers   Mitchell Lindgren, Tom Arthur,
                     & Rich McGowen

(opposite)
Design Firm **Dixon & Parcels Associates, Inc.**

   Client   The Bachman Company

1.

AESCULAP®

Navigator™

Surgical Management Systems

2.

GLENBOROUGH

3.

BUILDING CONFIDENCE

TRINITY

BUILDING MAINTENANCE

4.

6.

COMPUTER SYSTEMS DIVISION

NEC solutions

5.

powerware

Mercer

7.

8.

114

Crawford & Associates
I N T E R N A T I O N A L

The Power of Creative Learning℠

9.

10.

11.

12.

13.

14.

1.

2.

health quarters

your source for sexuality education and medical care

3.

CRESCENT
networks

4.

XyEnterprise™

5.

kallix

6.

E X P A N D
networks

7.

LEAGUESCHOOL

8.

116

9.

T·R·E·E·S

10.

MEXICO ℠ EXPRESS

Financial **Network**

11.

12.

Synapt
T E C H N O L O G I E S

CEATECH USA

13.

14.

Merrick
County

Breakers

15.

1 - 8			7. Designer	Aime Lecusay
	Design Firm	**Stewart Monderer Design, Inc.**	8. Client	League School of
9 - 13				Greater Boston
	Design Firm	**Raymond Wood/Design**	Designers	Aime Lecusay
14 - 15				& Stewart Monderer
	Design Firm	**Ron Bartels Design**		
			9. Client	The Tree People
1. Client		NBase/Xyplex	Designer	Raymond Wood
	Designers	Aime Lecusay		
		& Stewart Monderer	10. Client	Mexico Express
			Designer	Raymond Wood
2. Client		Dynisco		
	Designer	Stewart Monderer	11. Client	Boyd Communications
			Designer	Raymond Wood
3. Client		Health Quarters		
	Designer	Stewart Monderer	12. Client	Synapt Technologies
			Designer	Raymond Wood
4. Client		Crescent Networks		
	Designer	Aime Lecusay	13. Client	Ceatech USA
			Designer	Raymond Wood
5. Client		Xyvision Enterprise		
		Solutions, Inc.	14. Client	Center for Great Plains Studies
	Designer	Stewart Monderer	Designer	Ron Bartels
6. Client		Kallix Corporation	15. Client	Merrick County Sports
	Designer	Stewart Monderer	Designer	Ron Bartels

GRAEBE, DANNA & ASSOCIATES
THE RIGHT PATH FOR YOUR FINANCIAL FUTURE

1.

CENTER FOR LEADERSHIP DEVELOPMENT

2.

ISLAND
COMMUNICATIONS

3.

SUCCESS EXPRESS
A BRIDGE TO THE FUTURE

4.

NY·NJ·MPC,INC.

25th

ANNIVERSARY

5.

The New York Chinese Scholar's Garden

6.

singlish™

7.

(opposite)
Design Firm Onyx Design Inc.

Client Modern World Ventures Inc.
Designer Paul Morales

1 - 6
Design Firm Island Communications

7
Design Firm Philbrook & Associates

1. Client Graebe, Danna & Associates
    Designer Linda E. Danaher

2. Client Center for Leadership
             Development at Bristol-Myers
             Squibb Company
    Designer Linda E. Danaher

3. Client Island Communications
    Designer Linda E. Danaher

4. Client Success Express at Bristol-Myers
             Squibb Company
    Designer Linda E. Danaher

4. Client NY, NJ Minority
             Purchasing Council, Inc.
    Designer Linda E. Danaher

6. Client New York Chinese
             Scholar's Garden
    Designer Linda E. Danaher

7. Client Singlish Enterprises, Inc.
    Designer Bill Philbrook

1.

2.

3.

4.

5.

6.

7.

8.

9.

10.

11.

12.

13.

14.

15.

(all)

Design Firm DYNAPAC Design Group

1. Client   Advance Plastics
    Designers   Lee A. Aellig & Elsa Valdez

2. Client   DYNAPAC Design Group
    Designers   Lee A. Aellig, Marland Chow ,
                      & Angus R. Colson

3. Client   Dual Seat Technologies
    Designer   Lee A. Aellig

4. Client   Beyond Cool Tattoos
    Designer   Lee A. Aellig

5. Client   Heene Aaron's Plumbing
    Designer   Lee Aellig

6. Client   Hidden Meadow Foods
    Designer   Lee A. Aellig

7. Client   Micronetix Corporation
    Designer   Lee A. Aellig

8. Client   Mark Robinson
                      Income Tax Service
    Designer   Lee A. Aellig

9. Client   Calypso Artistic Imports
    Designers   Lee A. Aellig &
                      Robert Alexander

10. Client   Southwest Realtors
    Designer   Lee A. Aellig

11. Client   Mt. Helix Pest &
                      Termite Control
    Designer   Lee A. Aellig

12. Client   ProServices, Inc.
    Designer   Lee A. Aellig

13. Client   PhoneChip.com
    Designer   Lee A. Aellig

14. Client   The Voice Broadcasting
    Designer   Lee A. Aellig

15. Client   San Diego Real Estate Associates
    Designer   Lee A. Aellig

1.

2.

3.

4.

5.

visto.com™

life on the dot

6.

7.

1 - 6
Design Firm Onyx Design Inc.
7
Design Firm Primo Angeli Inc.

1. Client   Larkspur Hospitality Hotels
   Designers   Paul Morales & Dean Alvarez

2. Client   La Raza Centro legal
   Designer   Paul Morales

3. Client   Gilroy Foods/Con Agra
   Designers   Paul Morales & Dean Alvarez

4. Client   Caffe Marseille
   Designer   Paul Morales

5. Client   Riscorian Enterprise
   Designers   Dean Alvarez & Paul Morales

6. Client   Visto Corporation
   Designers   Dean Alvarez, Paul Morales,
                    & Wendy McPhee

7. Client   Informix/Software
   Designers   Paul Morales & Jeff Keogel

(opposite)
Design Firm Dynapac Design Group

   Client   C & H International
   Designers   Lee A. Aellig & Paula Hong

EUROPEAN
AVANTÁGE ™

1.

2.

3.

4.

EZ • METRICS

5.

6.

airia

7.

BERNARDINI CONSTRUCTION

8.

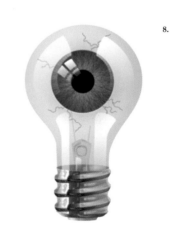

9.

10.

11.

12.

13.

AT THE MONARCH SPA

14.

TRAXSTAR

T E C H N O L O G I E S

15.

1 - 3		6. Client	Airia A Division of
Design Firm	Dean Alvarez Design		Flanders Filters
4 - 8		Designers	Gary W. Priester & Mark Husa
Design Firm	The Black Point Group		
9		7. Client	Bernardini Construction
Design Firm	Shields Design	Designers	Gary W. Priester
10 - 12			& Steve Bernardini
Design Firm	Balderman Creative Services		
13 - 15		8. Client	The Black Point Group
Design Firm	Creative Edge Design	Designer	Gary W. Priester
1. Client	Kimberly Aoki	9. Client	Maxim Mortgage Corporation
Designer	Dean Alvarez	Designer	Charles Shields
2. Client	Dean Alvarez Design	10. Client	Innovative Technologies
Designer	Dean Alvarez	Designer	Bobbi Balderman
3. Client	Plantation Pictures	11. Client	Balderman Creative Services
Designer	Dean Alvarez	Designer	Bobbi Balderman
4. Client	EZ Metrics, Foster Coburn	12. Client	Conceal-it
Designers	Gary W. Priester	Designer	Bobbi Balderman
	& Foster Coburn		
		13. Client	Bodylines
5. Client	i/us Corp., Arlen Bartch,	Designer	Cynthia Bancale
	Chris Dickman		
Designers	Gary W. Priester	14. Client	TraxStar Technologies
	& Chris Dickman	Designer	Chris Mohler
		15. Client	Healthtrac
		Designer	Cynthia Bancale

1.

SECURITY

2.

3.

4.

5.
HORIZON
NETWORK SOLUTIONS, INC.

6.

HamiltonInk

7.

8.

9.

10.

F I S H E R

11.

12.

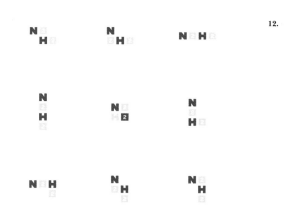

plan B™
(LEVONORGESTREL)

13.

14.

15.

Caldwell Industries, Inc.

2.

3.

4.

5.

AQUA-FLO
HYDRATION SYSTEM

6.

7.

(opposite)
Design Firm DYNAPAC Design Group

Client   Caldwell Industries, Inc.
Designer   Lee A. Aellig

1 - 7
Design Firm Laura Coe Design Assoc.

1. Client   Lumineux
    Designers   Laura Coe Wright
                & Leanne Leveillee

2. Client   Active Motif
    Designers   Ryoichi Yotsumoto
                & Laura Coe Wright

3. Client   Dataquick
    Designer   Ryoichi Yotsumoto

4. Client   Sea World of California
    Designers   Leanne Leveillee
                & Ryoichi Yotsumoto

5. Client   Taylor Made Golf Co.
    Designer   Ryoichi Yotsumoto

6. Client   Road Runner Sports
    Designer   Darryl Glass

7. Client   Road Runner Sports
    Designer   Ryoichi Yotsumoto

1.

Cerebix
Intelligent Information Solutions

2.

BESTSELLERS
BOOKS TO BEANS

3.

Rabbit Creek
TECHNOLOGY INC.

4.

A Catered Experience

5.

STEP 3 LTD

6.

NOODLE FACTORY
CHUN WAH KAM

7.

Bagel Bakers

8.

FOOD SOLUTIONS
UNIQUE CONVENIENT MEALS

UNITED WAY.
OF THE BAY AREA

9.

10.

UCSF STANFORD
HEALTH CARE

Stanford Hospital and Clinics

11.

Purple Moon™

12.

E*x*ponent™

13.

Cheskin
Research

14.

FUJIFILM
digital

15.

1 - 3		8. Client	Food Solutions
Design Firm Jansen Design		Designer	Nick Kaars
4 - 8			
Design Firm Nick Kaars Associates Inc.		9. Client	The United Way of the Bay Area
9 - 14		Designers	Mark Bergman
Design Firm SBG Enterprise			& Richard Patterson
15			
Design Firm Irwin Levine & Assoc.		10. Client	Flagstow Corp./Advantica Restaurant Group
		Designers	Mark Bergman & Tom Kane
1. Client	Cerebix		
Designer	Glenn Jansen	11. Client	UCSF Stanford
		Designers	Mark Bergman
2. Client	BestSellers		& Richard Patterson
Designer	Glenn Jansen		
		12. Client	Interval
3. Client	Rabbit Creek	Designers	Mark Bergman
Designer	Glenn Jansen		& Jessie McAnulty
4. Client	A Catered Experience	13. Client	Exponent
Designer	Nick Kaars	Designers	Mark Bergman & Amy Hershman
5. Client	Step 3		
Designer	Nick Kaars	14. Client	Cheskin Research
		Designers	Mark Bergman & Jessie McAnulty
6. Client	Chun Wah Kam Noodle Factory		
Designers	Darryl Soon & Nick Kaars	15. Client	Fuji Photo Film
		Designer	Brad Levine
7. Client	Bagel Bakers		
Designers	Oliver Kinney & Nick Kaars		

hothouse

digital

1.

2.

inhaus

3.

eliptica

4.

SOLARIAN

6.

5.

SLAVE

7.

ClassMate™

Curricular Management Software

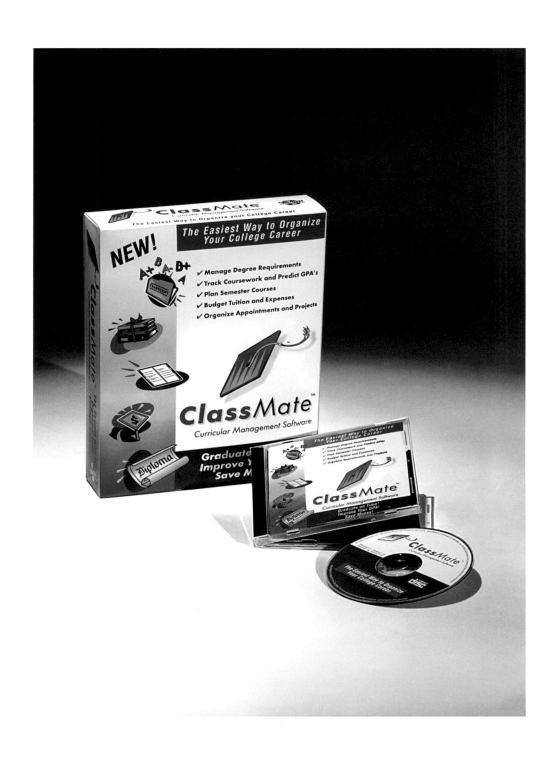

1.

AT&T

2.

HAL's
bar & grill

3.

NOMADIX

4.

medschool.com

5.

6.

HealthVest.com

7.

NetZero™

8.

NO. 9 RECORDS

9.

LA2012

10.

QORTET

11.

shipper.com

12.

13.

14.

Streamaster

15.

1 - 13
Design Firm Bright Strategic Design
14
Design Firm McNulty & Co.
15
Design Firm SBG Enterprises

1. Client   AT&T Corporation
    Designers   Keith Bright & Chad White

2. Client   Hal's Bar & Grill
    Designer   Keith Bright

3. Client   Nomadix
    Designers   Keith Bright & Weina Dinata

4. Client   Medschool.com
    Designers   Keith Bright & Stephanie Tsao

5. Client   Beverly Hills Farmers Market
    Designers   Keith Bright & Weina Dinata

6. Client   HealthVest.com
    Designers   Keith Bright & Weina Dinata

7. Client   Netzero Inc.
    Designers   Keith Bright & Stephanie Tsao

8. Client   No. 9 Records
    Designer   Keith Bright

9. Client   Los Angeles
                  Olympic Committee
    Designer   Keith Bright

10. Client   Qorus.com
    Designers   Keith Bright & Denis Parkhurst

11. Client   Shipper.com
    Designers   Keith Bright & Denis Parkhurst

12. Client   You Bet Racing Network
    Designers   Keith Bright, Matthew Bright,
                  & Richard Vasquez

13. Client   Direct Hit
    Designer   Keith Bright

14. Client   Motorola Streamaster
    Designers   Brian Jacobson & Dan McNulty

15. Client   Del Monte Foods
    Designer   Mark Bergman

135

1.

FirstEnergy
MILLENNIUM OF LIGHT
CLEVELAND 2000

2.

HORTON
35th
ANNIVERSARY

3.

Realty One | **Welcome Home**
Advantage
Program

4.

ArcAngel®

5.

P R E M I S E
COMMUNICATION SYSTEMS

6.

M I G I T E C H
hands-on training

7.

INTEGRATED
NETWORK
CONCEPTS

8.

digital
NAVIGATION

9.

10.

11.

12.

D²RM
Design/Development
Resource Management

13.

SATX

A Communication
Technologies
Company

14.

FURUTANI
USA · INC.

15.

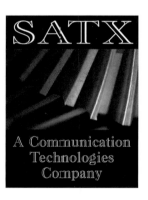

WOODSIDE
biomedical

1.

Torrey View

3.

4.

DOUBLE EAGLE

G O L F   C E N T E R

5.

sdps

6.

7.

Fine Furnishings and Design

CLASSIC INTERIORS

(opposite)
Design Firm DYNAPAC Design Group

Client   Woodside Biomedical, Inc.
Designer   Lee A. Aellig

1 - 7
Design Firm Conover

1. Client   Torrey View
    Designer   David Conover

2. Client   Classic Interiors
    Designers Amy Williams & David Conover

3. Client   Addison Homes
    Designer   David Conover

4. Client   Double Eagle
    Designer   David Conover

5. Client   Fraseworks
    Designer   David Conover

6. Client   Sejersen Digital
               Processing Services
    Designer   Carlos Avina

7. Client   El Dorado Stone
    Designers David Conover, Carlos Avina,
               & Amy Williams

1.

AVON
WOMEN OF
ENTERPRISE

AVON the company for women

2.

AVON
worldwide fund for
women's health

AVON the company for women

3.

AVON

4.

AVON
the company for women

5.

AVON

Women
inSight
Data base

6.

AVON
RUNNING

Global Women's Circuit

AVON the company for women

7.

AVON
PRODUCTS
FOUNDATION

AVON the company for women

8.

AVON
GLOBEX

GLOBAL EXCHANGE

AVON the company for women

9.

10.

MOUNT SINAI
SCHOOL OF
MEDICINE

11.

the acme **idea** company LLC

12.

CCG metaMEDIA inc

13.

14.

15.

(all)
Design Firm O & J Design, Inc.

1 - 8	Client	Avon Products, Inc.
Designers		Andrzej Olejniczak
		& Heishin Ra
9. Client		P. Wolfe Consultants, Inc.
Designer		Andrzej Olejniczak
10. Client		Mount Sinai School of Medicine
Designers		Barbara Olejniczak
		& Heishin Ra
11. Client		Avon Products, Inc.
Designers		Andrzej Olejniczak
		& Heishin Ra

12. Client		The Acme Idea Company
Designers		Barbara Olejniczak
		& Heishin Ra
13. Client		CCG MetaMedia, Inc.
Designers		Andrzej Olejniczak
		& Christina Mueller
14. Client		Consumers Interstate
		Corporation
Designers		Andrzej Olejniczak
		& Lia Camara-Mariscal
15. Client		Consumer Interstate
		Corporation
Designers		Andrzej Olejniczak
		& Lia Camara-Mariscal

1.

2.

3.

4.

5.

6.

ECHO
ROCK
VENTURES

7.

1 - 7
Design Firm   Clark Creative Group

1. Client   Big Wash
    Designers   Annemarie Clark & Craig Stout

2. Client   HuckleberryYouth Programs
    Designers   Annemarie Clark &
                  Ozzie Patton

3. Client   Siteline Communications Inc.
    Designers   Annemarie Clark & Craig Stout

4. Client   Sterling Consulting Group
    Designers   Annemarie Clark
                  & Thurlow Washam

5. Client   J. Eiting & Co.
    Designers   Annemarie Clark
                  & Carol Piechocki

6. Client   Echo Rock Ventures
    Designers   Annemarie Clark
                  & Thurlow Washam

7. Client   Hope Housing
    Designers   Annemarie Clark
                  & Hiroko Chastain

(opposite)
Design Firm   DYNAPAC Design Group

    Client   Experience Coffee
    Designer   Lee A. Aellig

EXPERIENCE COFFEE!

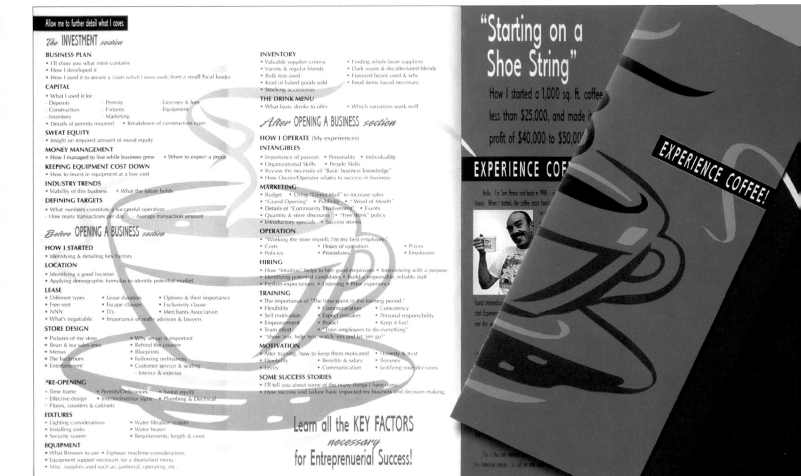

143

1.

2.

3.

4.

5.

6.

7.

8.

9.

10.

11.

12.

13.

14.

15.

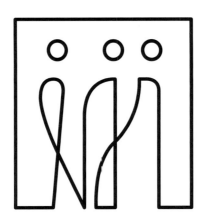

1 - 8
Design Firm EDAW, Inc.
9 - 11
Design Firm Ervin Marketing
            Creative Communications
12 - 13
Design Firm Julie Johnson Design
14
Design Firm Mires Design
15
Design Firm Doppelgänger, Inc.

1. Client   EDAW Corporate Logo
    Designer   Marty McGraw

2. Client   EDAW Principals Meeting 1998
    Designer   Marty McGraw

3. Client   EDAW Summer
                Student Program
    Designer   Marty McGraw

4. Client   EDAW Intranet
    Designer   Marty McGraw

5. Client   EDAW Human Resources Eye
    Designer   Marty McGraw

6. Client   EDAW Human Resources Hand
    Designer   Marty McGraw

7. Client   Kate Stickley
                Landscape Architect
    Designer   Marty McGraw

8. Client   RPR Architects
    Designer   Marty McGraw

9. Client   Brand Synergy
    Designer   Erica Schwan

10. Client   Visteon Information Technology/
                Ford Motor Company
    Designer   Erica Schwan

11. Client   Missouri Employers
                Mutual Insurance
    Designer   Jean Corea

12. Client   Mclean County Prenatal Clinic
    Designer   Julie Johnson

13. Client   Goldenleaf
    Designer   Julie Johnson

14. Client   Deleo Clay Tile Company
    Designer   José Serrano, Miguel Perez,
                & Dan Thoner

15. Client   Amana Corporation
    Designer   Otto Steininger

1.

Cellar Ideas

2.

Arena Cucina

Ravioli

HAND MADE BY FOUR ITALIAN WOMEN

3.

4.

5.

FAROUDJA
PICTURE PLUS

6.

Kibir!
IMAGING

7.

Mugsy's
COFFEE HOUSE & CIGAR CO.

8.

Silicon*Exchange*

9.

Syn*plicity*®

10.

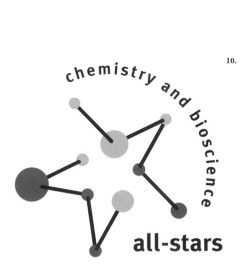

11.

12.

13.

14.

15.

1 - 11
Design Firm **Cellar Ideas**
12 - 14
Design Firm **McNulty & Co.**
15
Design Firm **SBG Enterprise**

1. Client	Cellar Ideas	8. Client	SGI: Silicon Exchange
Designer	Don Barnes	Designer	Don Barnes
2. Client	Arena Cucina	9. Client	Synplicity
Designer	Don Barnes	Designer	Don Barnes
3. Client	Proxim Symphony	10. Client	SGI: CBS all-stars
Designer	Don Barnes	Designer	Don Barnes
4. Client	Applied Materials: In Touch	11. Client	SGI: Son 2 work
Designer	Don Barnes	Designer	Don Barnes
5. Client	Faroudja Picture Plus	12. Client	Snow Summit
Designer	Don Barnes	Designer	Dan McNulty
6. Client	Kibir!	13. Client	People Support
Designer	Don Barnes	Designers	Brian Jacobson & Dan McNulty
7. Client	Mugsy's	14. Client	SMTEK International
Designer	Don Barnes	Designers	Eugene Bustillos & Dan McNulty
		15. Client	Cadbury Beverages, Inc.
		Designers	Mark Bergman & Jessie McAnulty

1.

CYTOVIA

2. virtrue

3.

StellarRoad

4.

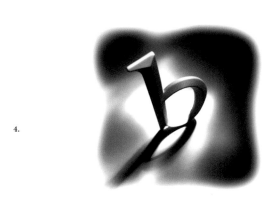

6.

PROCOM
TECHNOLOGY

5.

7.

1.

2.

3.

4.

5.

6.

7.

8.

150

COURY
ENTERPRISES
CONTRACTORS

9.

N E T W O R K S

10.

Alberstone Enterprises

11.

DiPrima
Insurance Specialists

12.

VcAf	VENTURA
	COUNTY
	ADVERTISING
	FEDERATION

13.

NYU
Orthopaedic Surgery

14.

NEW YORK UNIVERSITY
School of Continuing and
Professional Studies

15.

1 - 5
Design Firm be.
6 - 8
Design Firm DYNAPAC Design Group
9 - 13
Design Firm McNulty & Co.
14 - 15
Design Firm O & J Design, Inc.

1. Client   AdVerb
   Designer   Eric Read

2. Client   Devon
   Designers   Enrique Gaston & Eric Read

3. Client   Andresen
   Designer   Eric Read

4. Client   HP LaserJet Women's Challenge
   Designers   Will Burke & Yusuke Asaka

5. Client   be.
   Designers   Will Burke, Eric Read
               & Coralie Russo

6. Client   Specialty Fabric & Accessories
   Designer   Lee A. Aellig

7. Client   Casa De Maestas
   Designers   Lee A. Aellig & Jeff Maestas

8. Client   Innotech, LLC
   Designer   Lee A. Aellig

9. Client   Coury Enterprises
   Designers   Kristen Borg & Dan McNulty

10. Client   ACT Networks
    Designers Mark Luscombe & Dan McNulty

11. Client   Alberstone Enterprises
    Designers Mark Luscombe & Dan McNulty

12. Client   Di Prima Insurance
    Designers Eugene Bustillos & Dan McNulty

13. Client   Ventura County
               Advertising Federation
    Designer   Dan McNulty

14. Client   New York University,
               Hospital for Joint Diseases
    Designers Barbara Olejniczak & Heishin Ra

15. Client   New York University, School of
               Continuing & Professional Studies
    Designers Andrzej Olejniczak, Christina
               Mueller & Leslie Nayman

151

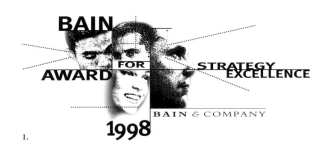

1.

2.

3.

4.

5.

6.

7.

1 - 7		
	Design Firm	Edward Walter Design, Inc.
8		
	Design Firm	Kym Abrams Design
9		
	Design Firm	Icon Graphics Inc.
10		
	Design Firm	Louey/Rubino Design Group, Inc.
11		
	Design Firm	Misha Design Studio
12		
	Design Firm	Festive Arts
13		
	Design Firm	Deutsch Design Works
14		
	Design Firm	Pisarkiewicz Mazur & Co., Inc.
15		
	Design Firm	Mickelson Design
1.	Client	Bain & Co.
	Designers	Edward Walter & Yuly Monsanto
2.	Client	Coopers & Lybrand's Human Resource Advisory
	Designer	Yuly Monsanto
3.	Client	Coopers & Lybrand ReservePro
	Designer	Martin Brynell
4.	Client	South Pacific Foods
	Designer	Edward Walter

5.	Client	Dub Rogers
	Designer	Edward Walter
6.	Client	Wise Solutions, Inc.
	Designer	Edward Walter
7.	Client	American Collectronix
	Designer	Edward Walter
8.	Client	Lovell & Whyte
	Designers	Amy Nathan & Kym Abrams
9.	Client	Wild Bird Center of America
	Designers	Icon Graphics Inc.
10.	Client	Tutto Bene
	Designer	Robert Louey
11.	Client	Temple Israel Synagogue
	Designer	Misha Lenn
12.	Client	Miziker & Company
	Designer	Lee Storey
13.	Client	Bammie Awards
	Designers	Barry Deutsch & Jess Biambroni
14.	Client	Town & Country Living Corp.
	Designer	Mary F. Pisarkiewicz
	Calligrapher	Genevieve Cerasoli
15.	Client	Anderson Auto
	Designer	Alan Mickelson

8.

9.

10.

11.

12.

13.

14.

15.

153

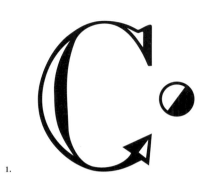

1.

2.

DOCERE

THE ALAN
GUTTMACHER
INSTITUTE
NEW YORK &
WASHINGTON

3.

4.

5.

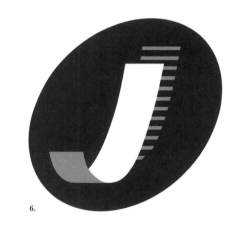

6.

Adult Literacy Media Alliance

7.

8.

154

9.

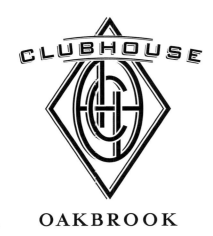

OAKBROOK

11.

10.

12.

D E N T A L   C A R E

13.

14.

15.

1 - 11
Design Firm   Edward Walter Design, Inc.
12 - 14
Design Firm   Clark Creative Group
15
Design Firm   SBG Enterprise

1. Client   Counterpoint
               Capital Management
   Designer   Per Evander

2. Client   Docere Studios
   Designer   Edward Walter

3. Client   The Alan Guttmacher Institute
   Designer   Martin Brynell

4. Client   El Mirasol Villas
   Designer   Martin Brynell

5. Client   Good Dog Press
   Designer   Edward Walter

6. Client   Jamestowm Packing + Display
   Designer   Manfred Junkert

7. Client   Alma
   Designer   Yuly Monsanto

8. Client   Computer Shopper Net Buyer
   Designer   Martin Brynell

9. Client   Prescient Energy Corp.
   Designer   Manfred Junkert

10. Client   Goller Productions Ink
    Designers Edward Walter & Yuly Monsanto

11. Client   The Clubhouse
    Designer   Edward Walter

12. Client   Oracle Corporation
    Designers Annemarie Clark
               & Thurlow Washam

13. Client   Dr. Baglio D.D.S.
    Designers Annemarie Clark & Kelly Clark

14. Client   Mayhem Productions
    Designer   Annemarie Clark

15. Client   Nestle, USA
    Designers Mark Bergman & Laura Cramer

155

1.

2.

TECHNOLOGY
DISTRIBUTOR PROGRAM

3.

4.

5.

6.

7.

8.

156

9.

10.

The CONTiNENTAL

11.

THE Contínental

12.

The NeXt Wave

13.

14.

The *Fitness Choice*

15.

1 - 4
Design Firm Graco Advertising
5 - 8
Design Firm Imagine That Design
9 - 15
Design Firm [i]e design

1, 2
   Client   Graco Industrial Division
   Designer   Gary Schmidt

3. Client   Contractor Equip Division,
                  Graco Inc
    Designer   Gary Schmidt

4. Client   Graco Automotive Division
    Designer   Gary Schmidt

5. Client   Chileen Painting
    Designer   Terry Austin

6. Client   Star Cleaning
    Designer   Terry Austin

7. Client   Imagine That Design
    Designer   Gary Schmidt

8. Client   Scharacon General Contractors
    Designer   Terry Austin

9. Client   Sunset Sound
    Designers   Marcie Carson, Mirjam Selmi,
                  & David Gilmour

10. Client   MediaPointe
    Designers   Cya Nelson & Marcie Carson

11. Client   The Continental
    Designer   Cya Nelson

12. Client   The Continental Olive Restaurant
    Designer   David Gilmour

13. Designer   David Gilmour

14. Client   Pool Boy
    Designer   Marcie Carson

15. Client   Fitness Choice
    Designers   Marcie Carson & David Gilmour

1.

2.

3.

4.

5.

6.

7.

1.

2.

3.

4.

5.

6.

7.

8.

9.

10.

11.

12.

13.

14.

PARENTS
ANONYMOUS

15.

(all)				
Design Firm	**GSD&M**			
		8.	Client	Heroes & Legacies Cigar Lounge
1.	Client	4empowerment.com		Designer	Brett Stiles
	Designer	Brett Stiles			
			9, 10		
2.	Client	Austin Film Festival		Client	Humane Society of Austin
	Designer	Brett Stiles		Designer	Brett Stiles
3.	Client	Concord Limousine Service	11.	Client	KAOS Hair Salon
	Designer	Brett Stiles		Designer	Brett Stiles
4.	Client	Cyberway Waterways	12.	Client	La Zona Rosa
	Designer	Brett Stiles		Designer	Brett Stiles
5.	Client	Fin Gear	13.	Client	LIM Research
	Designer	Brett Stiles		Designer	Brett Stiles
6.	Client	GlobalTrack	14.	Client	Parents Anonymous
	Designer	Brett Stiles		Designer	Brett Stiles
7.	Client	GSD&M	15.	Client	Peace Council
	Designer	Brett Stiles		Designer	Brett Stiles

1.

2.

3.

cross
photography

4.

5.

Ayse Celem Design

6.

7.

1, 4
Design Firm Product 101
2, 3
Design Firm Rowan & Martin Design
5, 6
Design Firm Ayse Celem
7
Design Firm SBG Enterprises

1. Client   Happy Capitalist Productions
    Designer   Ayse Celem

2. Client   Airwalk-WalMart
    Designer   Ayse Celem

3. Client   Sportzine
    Designer   Ayse Celem

4. Client   Dave Cross Photography
    Designer   Ayse Celem

5. Client   Atwood Day Sail
    Designer   Ayse Celem

6. Client   Ayse Celem Design
    Designer   Ayse Celem

7. Client   The Coca-Cola Company
    Designers   Mark Bergman, Margaret Lee,
                  & Laura Cramer

(opposite)
Design Firm Cathey Associates, Inc.

    Client   Jwana Juice
    Designer   Isabel Campos

1.

belyea.

VANDER HOUWEN PUBLIC RELATIONS

2.

3.

4.

5.

veenendaal **cave**

6.

7.
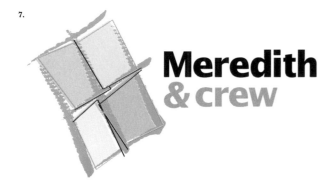

Meredith
& crew

UtilX®
EXPERTS IN UTILITY RENOVATION

8.

164

CruiseWest

9.

10.

11.

12.

Fulton Crossing
Paper Company

14.

MAISON DE FRANCE

13.

15.

GeoTrust SM

1 - 5, 7 - 15			8.	Client	UtilX
Design Firm	**Belyea**			Designers	Patricia Belyea
6					& Ron Lars Hansen
Design Firm	**Corporate Multimedia Design**		9.	Client	Cruise West
				Designers	Patricia Belyea
1.	Client	Belyea			& Ron Lars Hansen
	Designers	Patricia Belyea			
		& Ron Lars Hansen	10.	Client	International Dining Adventures
				Designers	Patricia Belyea & Christian Salas
2.	Client	VHPR			
	Designers	Patricia Belyea	11.	Client	Holland America
		& Ron Lars Hansen		Designers	Patricia Belyea
					& Ron Lars Hansen
3.	Client	Academy of Realist Art			
	Designers	Patricia Belyea & Christian Salas	12.	Client	Cruise West
				Designers	Patricia Belyea
4.	Client	Les Piafs			& Ron Lars Hansen
	Designers	Patricia Belyea & Christian Salas			
			13.	Client	Weyerhaeuser
5.	Client	Veenendaal Cave		Designers	Patricia Belyea
	Designers	Patricia Belyea			& Ron Lars Hansen
		& Anne Daugherty			
			14.	Client	Maison de France
6.	Client	Disabilities Awareness Issues		Designers	Patricia Belyea & Christian Salas
		Leaders Inc.			
	Designers	Norbert C. Saez & James Barry	15.	Client	GeoTrust
				Designers	Patricia Belyea
7.	Client	Meredith & Crew			& Ron Lars Hansen
	Designers	Patricia Belyea & Naomi Murphy			

1.

2.

3.

4.

5.

6.

7.

8.

9.

10.

11.

DIANE TUTCH
MANAGEMENT CONSULTANT

12.

13.

14.

15.

(all)
Design Firm Jeff Fisher LogoMotives

1. Client   Kay Johnson's Sing
                  Out Productions
    Designer   Jeff Fisher

2. Client   Oregon Dept. of
                  Environmental Quality
    Designers   Jeff Fisher & Marcia Danab

3, 4
    Client   James John School
    Designer   Jeff Fisher

5. Client   Frit Creek Gardens
    Designer   Jeff Fisher

6. Client   W.B. Wells & Associates
    Designers   Jeff Fisher & Esther Lorance

7. Client   Virtual Office
    Designer   Jeff Fisher

8. Client   Queen Anne Royals
    Designer   Jeff Fisher

9. Client   Portland Trail Blazers
    Designers   Jeff Fisher & Sara Perrin

10. Client   Seattle Seahawks
    Designers   Jeff Fisher & Sara Perrin

11. Client   Joy Creek Nursery
    Designer   Jeff Fisher

12. Client   Diane Tutch
    Designer   Jeff Fisher

13. Client   Kristin & Tim Kelly
    Designer   Jeff Fisher

14. Client   Sisters Reride Association
    Designer   Jeff Fisher

15. Client   Website Today
    Designer   Jeff Fisher

HERITAGE CENTER

1.

2.

Nylon Plastics and Polymers by **Solutia**

3.

Quality Products. Exceptional Response.

4.

5.

6.

www.goinet.com

7.

(opposite)
Design Firm Walsh & Associates, Inc.

Client   Chugach Heritage
              Center/Alaska
Designer   Miriam Lisco

1 - 7
Design Firm Stan Gellman
**   Graphic Design Inc.**

1. Client   Buckingham Asset Management
    Designers   Chris Reifschneider
                & Barry Tilson

2. Client   Miller Management
    Designers   Barry Tilson & Erin Goter

3. Client   Solutia
    Designers   Barry Tilson & Jill Lampen

4. Client   Astaris
    Designers   Mike Donovan & Barry Tilson

5. Client   1999 National
                Governor's Association
    Designers   Mike Donovan & Barry Tilson

6. Client   Promotional Consultants/
                The Peernet Group
    Designers   Barry Tilson & Mike Donovan

7. Client   Goinet
    Designers   Erin Goter & Barry Tilson

1.

2.

3.

SECOND
BAPTIST
CHURCH

4.

SHARPS COMPLIANCE INC.

5.

Med Synergies

Communicating at the speed of now!

6.

7.

Integrated
Electrical
Services

8.

the **council** on
alcohol and **drugs**
houston

170

Cornerstone Solutions

centegra™

COALITION
OF BEHAVIORAL
HEALTH SERVICES

GOURMET COFFEES
BENGAL
TRADERS

ASSOCIATED COUNSEL *of* AMERICA ℠

Oiltanking

RESOURCENTER

(all)

Design Firm	**Loucks & Johnson**	
1. Client	USA Cafe	
Designers	Tim Johnson & Jay Loucks	
2. Client	Steverson Staffing Services	
Designers	Tim Johnson & Jay Loucks	
3. Client	Second Baptist Church	
Designers	Tim Johnson & Jay Loucks	
4. Client	Sharps Compliance	
Designers	Tim Johnson & Jay Loucks	
5. Client	MedSynergies	
Designers	Tim Johnson & Jay Loucks	
6. Client	InfoHighway	
Designers	Tim Johnson & Jay Loucks	
7. Client	Integrated Electrical Services	
Designers	Tim Johnson & Jay Loucks	

8. Client	The Council on Alcohol and Drugs
Designers	Tim Johnson & Jay Loucks
9. Client	Cornerstone Solutions
Designers	Tim Johnson & Jay Loucks
10. Client	Centegra
Designers	Tim Johnson & Jay Loucks
11. Client	Coalition of Behavioral Health Services
Designers	Tim Johnson & Jay Loucks
12. Client	Exxon
Designers	Tim Johnson & Jay Loucks
13. Client	Associated Counsel of America
Designers	Tim Johnson & Jay Loucks
14. Client	Oiltanking
Designers	Tim Johnson & Jay Loucks
15. Client	Resource Center
Designers	Tim Johnson & Jay Loucks

1.

Seattle Children's
home

2.

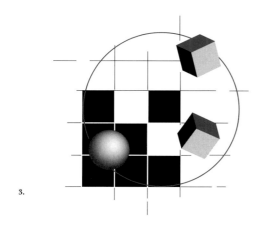

3.

R O B E R T
S C R I B N E R

4.

**GageTalker
CimWorks**

5.

SAKSON & TAYLOR

6.

7.

1 - 6
Design Firm Walsh & Associates
7
Design Firm SBG Enterprise

1. Client   Reflex Communications
    Designers   Mark Ely & Miriam Lisco

2. Client   Seattle Children's Home
    Designer   Miriam Lisco

3. Client   Parker Le Pla,
                  Brand Development
    Designer   Miriam Lisco

4. Client   Robert Scribner Salon
    Designers   Miriam Lisco & Glen Yoshiyama

5. Client   GageTalker CimWorks
    Designer   Miriam Lisco

6. Client   Sakson & Taylor
    Designer   Miriam Lisco

7. Client   Excel Corp.
    Designer   Mark Bergman

(opposite)
    Design Firm Walsh & Associates, Inc.

    Client   PC Fixx
    Designer   Miriam Lisco

1.

2.

3.

4.

5.

6.

7.

8.
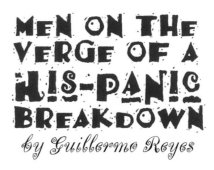

174

9.

10.

11.

12.

13.

14.

15.

(all)
Design Firm Jeff FisherLogoMotives

1 - 15
Client   triangle productions!
Designer   Jeff Fisher

1.

2.

3.

4.

5.

6.

7.

8.

9.

24~27 June 2001   San Antonio, Texas

10.

Insurance Rating Systems, Inc.
Agency Information Management System

11.

12.

13.

14.

15.

1
Design Firm SBG Enterprises
2 - 15
Design Firm Creative Link Studio, Inc.

1. Client   Autodesk
    Designers   Mark Bergman, Richard
                  Patterson & Iratxe Mumford

2. Client   San Antonio Spurs/
                  Harley Silent Auction
    Designers   Mark Broderick, Kyle Derr,
                  & Kevin La Rue

3. Client   Carti Paper Sculptures
    Designers   Kyle Derr, Kevin La Rue,
                  & Mark Broderick

4. Client   Racquetball & Fitness Clubs
    Designers   Kyle Derr, Kevin La Rue,
                  & Mark Broderick

5. Client   Global Scape
    Designers   Kyle Derr, Mark Broderick,
                  & Kevin La Rue

6. Client   Kids Sports Network
    Designers   Kyle Derr, Mark Broderick, &
                  Kevin La Rue

7. Client   Production Crew
    Designers   Kyle Derr, Kevin La Rue,
                  & Mark Broderick

8. Client   My Free LD.com
    Designers   Kyle Derr, Kevin La Rue
                  & Mark Broderick

9. Client   Kids Sports Network
    Designers   Kyle Derr, Mark Broderick,
                  & Kevin LaRue

10. Client   Rotary International
    Designers   Mark Broderick, Kyle Derr,
                  & Kevin LaRue

11. Client   IRS-AIMS
    Designers   Kevin LaRue, Mark Broderick,
                  & Kyle Derr

12. Client   Communications Arts Society
                  of San Antonio
    Designers   Mark Broderick, Kevin LaRue,
                  & Kyle Derr

13. Client   Special Olympics Texas
    Designers   Kyle Derr, Kevin LaRue,
                  & Mark Broderick

14. Client   Dads Day.com
    Designers   Kyle Derr, Kevin LaRue,
                  & Mark Broderick

15. Client   Global Scape Products
    Designers   Kyle Derr, Kevin LaRue,
                  & Mark Broderick

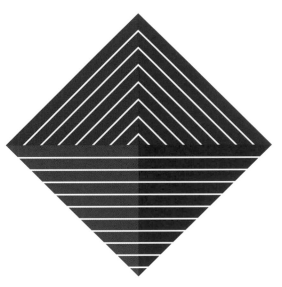

Advanced Network
Technologies, Inc.

1.

2.

3.

4.

5.

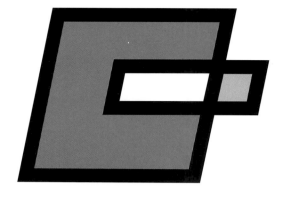

6.

7.

Bloom Smith
Landscape Rejuvenation ▪ Design & Installation

(opposite)
Design Firm Cathey Associates, Inc.

Client   Advanced Network
                  Technologies, Inc.
Designer   Gordon Cathey

1 - 5
**Design Firm Visual Marketing
              Associates, Inc.**
6
Design Firm Lori Powell Design Exploration
7
Design Firm Cathey Associates, Inc.

1. Client   Telestar Interactive Corporation
   Designer   Tom Davie

2. Client   CYND Snowboard Apparel
   Designer   Jason Selke

3. Client   Heartland Airlines
   Designer   Lynn Sampson

4. Client   Columbus Zoo
   Designer   Tom Davie

5. Client   Aullwood Audubon Center
                  and Farm
   Designer   Michael Butts

6. Client   Bridgeway Capital
   Designer   Lori Powell

7. Client   BloomSmith
   Designer   Matt Westapher

1.

2.

3.

Citizens
for Traffic
Solutions

4.

5.

6.

nQuest

7.

Foundation Labs

8.

R E G I O N

9.

DLush

10.

Potomac Marine

11.

National AIDS Marathon Training Program

12.

GourmetLuxe ®

13.

encoding.com

14.

MULVANNY
ARCHITECTS

15.

1 - 3
Design Firm Kollberg/Johnson
4 - 12
Design Firm Blank
13 - 15
Design Firm Walsh & Associates, Inc.

1. Client   Ambi Inc.
   Designers   Kollberg/Johnson

2. Client   Red Rooster Tobacconist
   Designer   Gary Kollberg

3. Client   Brooklyn Bottling
   Designer   Eileen Strauss

4. Client   end gridlock.com
   Designers   Robert Kent Wilson
               & Susan Burch Ahlers

5. Client   e student loan
   Designers   Robert Kent Wilson
               & Suzanne Ultman

6. Client   Red Hat Software
   Designers   Robert Kent Wilson, Suzanne
               Ultman & Adam Cohn

7. Client   Natural Question Technology
   Designer   Robert Kent Wilson

8. Client   Foundation Labs
   Designer   Robert Kent Wilson

9. Client   Responsible Economic Growth
               In Our Nation
   Designer   Robert Kent Wilson

10. Client   Dlush
    Designers Robert Kent Wilson
               & Suzanne Ultman

11. Client   Potomac Marine
    Designer   Robert Kent Wilson

12. Client   Walk the Talk Productions
    Designers Robert Kent Wilson, Suzanne
               Ultman & Adam Cohn

13. Client   GourmetLuxe
    Designer   Miriam Lisco

14. Client   Encoding.com
    Designers Mark Ely & Miriam Lisco

15. Client   Mulvanny Architects
    Designers Lyn Blanchard &Miriam Lisco

1.

perrydesign

2.

The Aurora Group
Manufacturers' Representatives

3.

 LiRA Enterprises

4.

ims
INTEGRATED MIDI SYSTEMS

5.

JN
music

6.

CANCER care®

7.

L b

Lieber Brewster Design, Inc.

1 - 5
Design Firm Perry Design
6 -7
Design Firm Lieber Brewster Design, Inc.

1. Client   Perry Design
    Designer   Kim Perry

2. Client   The Aurora Group
    Designer   Kim Perry

3. Client   Lira Enterprises
    Designers   Kim Perry & Kenneth DiPaola

4. Client   Integrated Midi Systems
    Designer   Kim Perry

5. Client   JN Music
    Designer   Kim Perry

6. Client   Cancer Care
    Designers   Elisa Carson & Anna Lieber

7. Client   Lieber Brewster Design, Inc.
    Designer   Anna Lieber

(opposite)
Design Firm Zunda Design Group

    Client   Newman's Own Inc.
    Designers   Jon Voss & Charles Zunda

182

183

1.

2.

3.

4.

5.

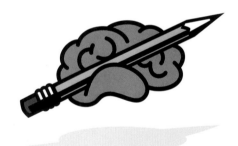

6.

7.

8.

9.

10.

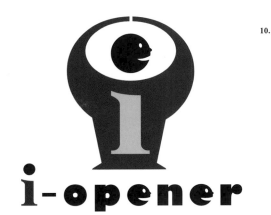

i-opener

11.

12.

Netpliance

13.

SHRED DOC ®

14.

WE'RE TEXAS

15.

MLK 2000

(all) Design Firm GSD&M		
1. Client	Pebble Beach	
Designer	Brett Stiles	
2. Client	Ranger Construction	
Designer	Brett Stiles	
3. Client	Texas Monthly	
Designer	Brett Stiles	
4. Client	TMW Group	
Designer	Brett Stiles	
5. Client	Words & Music	
Designer	Brett Stiles	
6. Client	Write Brain Works	
Designer	Brett Stiles	
7. Client	Agilion	
Designer	Craig Denham	

8. Client	Doubletree Hotel
Designer	Craig Denham
9. Client	Fort Worth Zoo
Designer	Craig Denham
10. Client	i-opener
Designer	Craig Denham
11. Client	Mother's Choice/Wal-Mart
Designer	Craig Denham
12. Client	Netpliance
Designer	Craig Denham
13. Client	Shred Doc
Designer	Craig Denham
14. Client	University of Texas
Designer	Craig Denham
15. Client	Austin Area Heritage Council
Designer	Kevin Peake

185

1.

2.

3.

4.

5.

6.

7.

8.

9.

10.

11.

12.

13.

Architecture for Computing Infrastructures and Networks

14.

15.

(all)			
Design Firm	**Jeff Fisher LogoMotives**		
1. Client	triangle productions!	8. Client	Pacific Association of College Registrars and Admissions Officers
Designer	Jeff Fisher	Designer	Jeff Fisher
2, 3			
Client	triangle productions!/ Stark Raving Theatre	9. Client	A Rubber's Ducky
Designer	Jeff Fisher	Designer	Jeff Fisher
4. Client	Shleifer Marketing Communications (Rutherford Investment Management)	10. Client	Shleifer Marketing Communications (American Telecom)
		Designer	Jeff Fisher
Designer	Jeff Fisher	11. Client	Dan Anderson Homes
5. Client	Oregon Adult Soccer Association		Designer	Jeff Fisher
		12. Client	AMP/Anne-Marie Petrie
Designer	Jeff Fisher	Designer	Jeff Fisher
6. Client	Oregon Adult Soccer Association	13. Client	Archinetix
		Designer	Jeff Fisher
Designer	Jeff Fisher	14. Client	Smith Freed Heald & Chock
7. Client	Pacific Association of College Registrars and Admissions Officers		Designer	Jeff Fisher
		15. Client	Spirit Expressing
Designer	Jeff Fisher	Designer	Jeff Fisher

188

1.

HEIDI GILMORE

2.

CORPORATE INTERNET SERVICES

3.

AN EVENT FOR EVERY AGE
DINOSAUR
DASH
FRIENDS OF MILWAUKEE PUBLIC MUSEUM

clothing accessories jewelry

4.

6.

GRAPHICSOURCE
PRODUCTION/FULFILLMENT

5.

7.

FRAMING AMY

(opposite)
Design Firm Zunda Design Group

Client   Bestfoods Baking
Designer   Charles Zunda

1, 3 - 7
Design Firm Becker Design
2
Design Firm Cathey Associates, Inc.

1. Client   Heidi Gilmore
    Designer   Neil Becker

2. Client   Virtual Line
    Designer   Gordon Cathey

3. Client   Friends of the Milwaukee
                 Public Museum
    Designer   Neil Becker

4. Client   Garbs
    Designer   Neil Becker

5. Client   Its Something Blue.com
    Designer   Neil Becker

6. Client   Graphicsource
    Designer   Neil Becker

7. Client   Framing Amy
    Designer   Neil Becker

189

1.

2.

3.

4.

5.

6.

7.

8.

9.

10.

11.

12.

13.

tech*Agent*

14.

THE GATHERING

15.

(all)

Design Firm   Imagine Graphics

1. Client   The Mortgage Network
    Designer   Steve Guy

2. Client   Almaden Press
    Designer   Steve Guy

3. Client   Nat'l Assoc. of Missions Pastors
    Designer   Steve Guy

4. Client   Nevada Institute for
                 Money Management
    Designer   Steve Guy

5. Client   Rocky Mountain Soda Company
    Designer   Steve Guy

6. Client   South Valley Christian Church
    Designer   Kyle Maxwell

7. Client   The Creeks Alzheimer's
                 & Dementia Care Ctrs.
    Designer   Kyle Maxwell

8. Client   First Baptist Church of Los Altos
    Designer   Kyle Maxwell

9. Client   TastyH$_2$O.com
    Designer   Steve Guy

10. Client   ViLink
    Designer   Steve Guy

11. Client   Integrated Financial
    Designers   Steve Guy & Kyle Maxwell

12. Client   Church of God of San Jose
    Designer   Kyle Maxwell

13. Client   Tech-Agent, Inc.
    Designer   Steve Guy

14 - 15
    Client   South Valley Christian Church
    Designer   Kyle Maxwell

SwigBurris

1.

2.

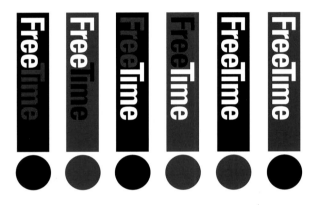

3.

MEC GROUP

4.

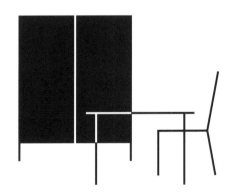

5.

6.

2D+T

7.

1 - 7
Design Firm Red Square Design

1. Client   Swig Burris
    Designer   Nadine Hajjar

2. Client   Cedar Corp.
    Designers   Lev Zeitlin & Nadine Hajjar

3. Client   Free Time
    Designer   Lev Zeitlin

4. Client   Middle East Capital Group
    Designers   Lev Zeitlin & Nadine Hajjar

5. Client   Borja Veciana
    Designer   Lev Zeitlin

6. Client   Société Moderne D'Enterprise
                  et de commerce (SMEC)
    Designer   Lev Zeitlin

7. Client   Two Dresses and a Tripod
    Designer   Lev Zeitlin

(opposite)
Design Firm Walsh & Associates

    Designers   Miriam Lisco, Iskra Johnson
                  & Mark Ely

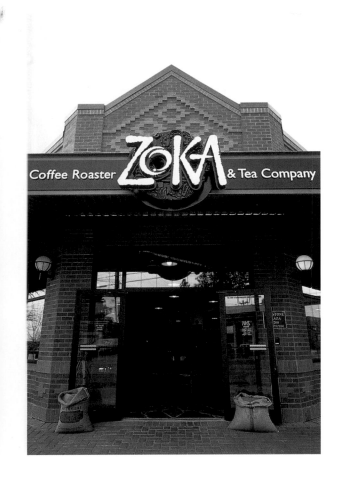

1.

2.

GroupWyse

Working Together Wisely

3.

4.

5.

6.

MERRY HAVEN

HEALTH CARE CENTER

7.

8.

9.

Puget Sound Trading

10.

Women's Imaging & Breast Health Center

11.

GRADUATE SCHOOL OF BUSINESS

CELEBRATING **20** YEARS

DOMINICAN UNIVERSITY

12.

steel wool] design

13.

OKNO TECHNOLOGIES

14.

OIL CAPITAL ELECTRIC

15.

CAVION™

CARE MANAGEMENT SYSTEM

1 - 10
Design Firm Graphx Design
11 - 14
Design Firm Steel Wool Design
15
Design Firm Becker Design

1. Client   Buyken Metal Products
   Designers Alex Sobie & Kari Baker

2. Client   GroupWyse
   Designers Alex Sobie & Patrick Smith

3. Client   DCS Decor
   Designers Alex Sobie, Kari Baker,
   & Patrick Smith

4. Client   Inn at Lake Connamarra
   Designers Kari Baker & Kaycia Ogata

5. Client   Jet City Bistro
   Designer Kari Baker

6. Client   Merry Haven
   Designers Kari Baker & Donna Cooley

7. Client   Natural Dental
   Designers Kari Baker & Donna Cooley

8. Client   Paradigm Search & Consulting
   Designers Alex Sobie & Patrick Smith

9. Client   Puget Sound Trading
   Designers Alex Sobie & Kari Baker

10. Client   Washington Imaging
    Services, LLC
    Designer Kari Baker

11. Client   Dominican University
    Designer Kristy Lewis Andrew

12. Client   Steel Wool Design
    Designer Kristy Lewis Andrew

13. Client   OKNO Technologies
    Designer Kristy Lewis Andrew

14. Client   Oil Capital Electric
    Designer Kristy Lewis Andrew

15. Client   Cavion
    Designers Neil Becker

1.

2.

HOSPICE OF
HUMBOLDT

3.

THE EVERY
KID FUND

4.

commission on
children
families &
community

5.

DIVERSITY
NETWORK

6.

KidStuff
PUBLIC RELATIONS

7.

PEGGY
SUNDAYS

8.

Fall Thesis Students
REED COLLEGE 1997

9.

10.

11.

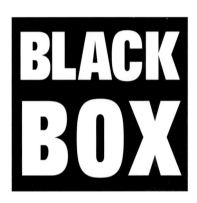

BLACK BOX

12.

BEIRUT
A 21ST CENTURY LOVE STORY

13.

The
ARCHIVES
R·O·O·M

14.

The
AIDS
MEMORIAL
R·O·O·M
A Living Room for Us All

15.

(all)
Design Firm Jeff Fisher LogoMotives

1.	Client	Peninsula Clean Team	6.	Client	DiversityNetwork
	Designer	Jeff Fisher		Designer	Jeff Fisher
2.	Client	Salvation Army/Moore St. Temple Corps	7.	Client	KidStuff Public Relations
	Designer	Jeff Fisher		Designer	Jeff Fisher
3.	Client	Hospice of Humboldt	8.	Client	Peggy Sundays
	Designer	Jeff Fisher		Designer	Jeff Fisher
4.	Client	TriAd (The Every Kid Fund)	9, 10	Client	Reed College
	Designers	Jeff Fisher & Sue Fisher		Designer	Jeff Fisher
5.	Client	Commission on Children, Families & Community	11 - 15	Client	triangle productions!
	Designer	Jeff Fisher		Designer	Jeff Fisher

198

1.

2.

3.

4.

5.

6.

7.

(opposite)
Design Firm Zunda Design Group

Client   Hershey Chocolate U.S.A.
Designers   Jon Voss & Charles Zunda

1.
Design Firm Red Square Design
2 - 7
Design Firm Becker Design

1. Client   Al Bustan
    Designers   Lev Zeitlin & Nadine Hajjar

2. Client   About Face
    Designer   Neil Becker

3. Client   Hunter Coaching
                and Consulting
    Designers   Neil Becker, Lisa Gaertig

4. Client   King Financial
    Designer   Neil Becker

5. Client   CUNA Brokerage Services, Inc.
    Designer   Neil Becker

6. Client   Zoom Messenger, llc
    Designer   Neil Becker

7. Client   Milwaukee Ballet
    Designer   Neil Becker

1.

2.

3.

4.

5.

6.

7.

8.

9.

MANGIA

10.

11.

12.

SCRATCH OFFS
— TEXAS LOTTERY —

13.

14.

TEXAS
MILLION
— TEXAS LOTTERY —

15.

(all)
Design Firm GSD&M

1. Client   City of Austin
    Designers   Marty Erhart & Tim McClure

2. Client   GSD&M
    Designers   Marty Erhart & Heather Segrest

3. Client   Jewish Family Service
    Designer   Marty Erhart

4. Client   Star of Texas Fair & Rodeo
    Designer   Patrick Nolan

5, 6
    Client   Chili's Grill & Bar
    Designer   Matt Mason

7. Client   Chili's Grill & Bar
    Designers   Matt Mason & Paul Rogers

8. Client   Dr. Larry "Hoppy" Lane, Dentist
    Designer   Matt Mason

9. Client   Frio Canyon Lodge
    Designer   Matt Mason

10. Client   Mangia Pizza
    Designer   Matt Mason

11. Client   Mason's Pit Stop Sauce
    Designer   Matt Mason

12. Client   Southwest Airlines
    Designer   Matt Mason

13, 14
    Client   Texas Lottery Commission
    Designer   Matt Mason

15. Client   Hill Country Ride for AIDS
    Designer   Marty Erhart

201

1.

2.

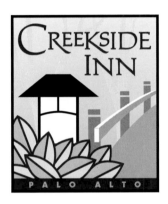

3.

4.

5.

6.

7.

1.

2.

SYNTONICS

3.

KENNEDY CONSULTING LLC

4.

Cox Design Group llc

5.

namasté

6.

ProSourcing

A Beers & Cutler Company

7.

Jagtiani+Associates

Protecting your ideas

8.

9.

10.

12.

11.

w e b
television

SAYLORS
Dental Laboratory, Inc.

13.

Pfeiffer®

14.

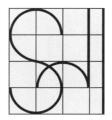

Reward®

15.

1 - 8, 11 - 13
Design Firm Fuller Designs, Inc.
9
Design Firm Swieter Design
10
Design Firm Frank D'Astolfo Design
14 - 15
Design Firm Chesapeake Group, Inc.

1. Client   Greenbrier School
   Designer   Doug Fuller

2. Client   Reston Community Center
   Designers   Doug Fuller & Aaron Taylor

3. Client   Syntonics
   Designers   Doug Fuller & Aaron Taylor

4. Client   Kennedy Consulting
   Designer   Minh Ta

5. Client   Cox Design Group
   Designer   Doug Fuller

6. Client   Namasté
   Designer   Doug Fuller

7. Client   Pro Sourcing
   Designer   Doug Fuller

8. Client   Jagtiani + Associates
   Designer   Doug Fuller

9. Client   Verve
   Designer   Mark Ford

10. Client   Simulprobe Technologies
    Designer   Frank D'Astolfo

11. Client   Global Systems & Strategies
    Designer   Doug Fuller

12. Client   J-Web Television
    Designer   Doug Fuller

13. Client   Saylors Dental Laboratory
    Designer   Minh Ta

14. Client   T. Marzetti Company
    Designer   John C. Sullivan

15. Client   Heinz Pet Products
    Designers Tina Collin & John C. Sullivan

1.

2.

Childpeace

MONTESSORI COMMUNITY

3.

4.

5.

6.

7.

8.

9.

10.

Classic Style for Hair and Nails

11.

12.

13.

14.

15.

1 - 15
Design Firm Jeff Fisher LogoMotives

1. Client	Portsmouth Community Development Corporation	8. Client	Dorene Cantrall Fisher
Designer	Jeff Fisher	Designer	Jeff Fisher
2. Client	Junior League of Portland	9. Client	Balloons on Broadway
Designer	Jeff Fisher	Designer	Jeff Fisher
3. Client	Childpeace Montessori Community	10. Client	Co•Motion Cycles
Designer	Jeff Fisher	Designers	Jeff Fisher & Jerril Nilson
4. Client	Oregon Daily Emerald	11. Client	Diva
Designer	Jeff Fisher	Designer	Jeff Fisher
5. Client	Janet Loughrey Horticulture Photography	12. Client	Pride Northwest, Inc.
Designer	Jeff Fisher	Designer	Jeff Fisher
6. Client	Jeff Fisher LogoMotives	13. Client	Rob Buckmaster Fund
Designer	Jeff Fisher	Designer	Jeff Fisher
7. Client	Kimberly Webster	14. Client	Our House of Portland
Designer	Jeff Fisher	Designer	Jeff Fisher
		15. Client	Greater Palm Springs Pride, Inc.
		Designer	Jeff Fisher

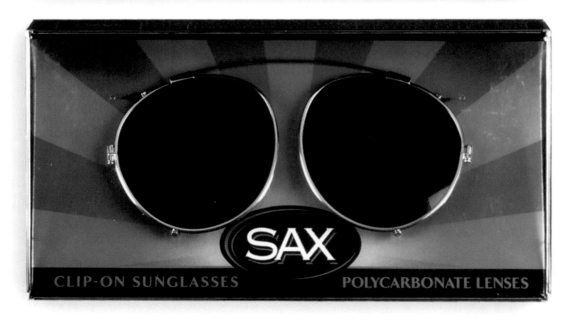

1.

2.

3.

4.

5.

6.

7.

(opposite)
Design Firm   Zunda Design Group

Client   Sax
Designers   Charles Zunda & Todd Nickel

1 - 7
Design Firm   Bartels & Company, Inc.

1. Client   The Crown Awards
    Designers   Ron Rodemacher
                 & David Bartels

2. Client   Benz Press Werks
    Designers   Bob Thomas & David Bartels

3. Client   City Coffee House
    Designer   John Postlewait

4. Client   Newco, Inc.
    Designers   David Bartels &
                 Ron Rodemacher

5. Client   Cheap Smokes
    Designers   John Postlewait & David Bartels

6. Client   Cybermill
    Designers   David Bartels &
                 Ron Rodemacher

7. Client   Holy Redeemer Church
    Designers   Ron Rodemacher &
                 David Bartels

J J GUMBERG CO.

2.

VICTORIA + CO

1.

3.

4.

5.

6.

7.

8.

LUX ART INSTITUTE

Shaw's
COFFEE LTD

7. Client   National Reprographics, Inc.
   Designers   Douglas Morris &
               L. Richard Poulin

1 - 4, 6 - 8
Design Firm Poulin + Morris
5
Design Firm Swieter Design
9 - 13
Design Firm Mires Design
14 - 15
Design Firm Bartels & Co., Inc.

8. Client   Planned Expansion Group Inc.
   Designer   Douglas Morris

9. Client   G.ball.com
   Designers   Scott Mires, Miguel Perez,
               & Tracy Sabin

1. Client   J. J. Gumberg Co
   Designers   L. Richard Poulin
               & Jonathan Posnett

10. Client   Arena Stage
    Designers Scott Mires & Miguel Perez

2. Client   Victoria + Co
   Designers   Douglas Morris &
               L. Richard Poulin

11. Client   Hell Racer
    Designers José Serrano, Miguel Perez,
               & Dan Thoner

3. Client   GSO Graphics Inc.
   Designers   Douglas Morris &
               Robert Patrick Festino

12. Client   Schiedermayer & Assoc.
    Designers José Serrano, Jeff Samaripa,
               & Miguel Perez

4. Client   Ridgeway Center
   Designer   Douglas Morris

13. Client   Lux Art Institute
    Designers John Ball & Miguel Perez

5. Client   The Dr. Benjamin Remedy

14. Client   Magna Bank
    Designers Ron Rodemacher
               & David Bartels

6. Client   Bratskeir + Company
   Designers   Douglas Morris &
               L. Richard Poulin

15. Client   Shaw's Coffee Ltd.
    Designer   Brian Barclay

1.

2.

Lightship

4.

3.

6.

WE'RE GOING PLACES

5.

7.

1 - 5
Design Firm Q. Cassetti
6 - 7
Design Firm Look

1. Client   Omega One Communications
    Designer   Q. Cassetti

2. Client   Lightship Telecom LLC
    Designer   Q. Cassetti

3. Client   Quest Diagnostics Incorporated
    Designer   Q. Cassetti

4. Client   Corning Museum of Glass
    Designers   Q. Cassetti & Rob Cassetti

5. Client   Corning Museum of Glass
    Designers   Q. Cassetti & Rob Cassetti

6. Client   Premiere, Limousine Company
    Designer   Betsy Todd

7. Client   Sea Breeze Preschool
    Designer   Betsy Todd

(opposite)
Design Firm DYNAPAC DesignGroup

Client   Advance Plastics
Designer   Lee A. Aellig

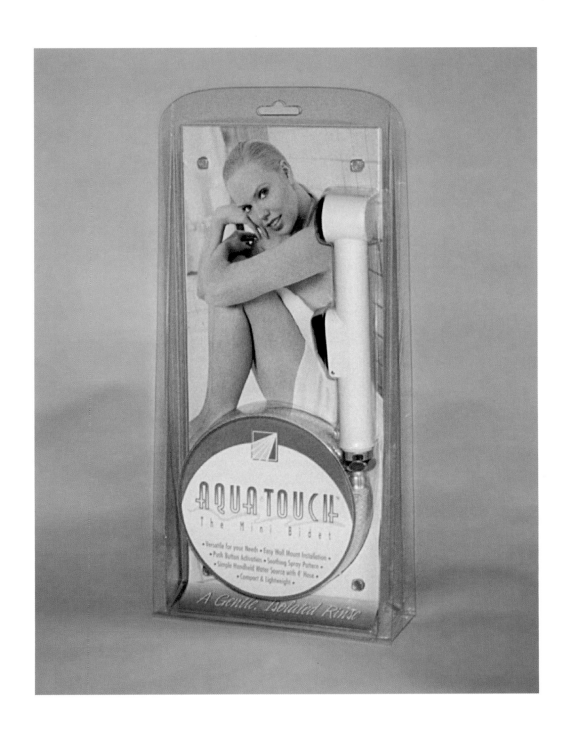

1.

JUST
THINK
FOUNDATION

2.

3.

SEA BREEZE SCHOOL
RICHES
OF THE
RAIN
FOREST

4.

VANCE BROWN
BUILDERS

5.

6.

7.

EXECUTIVES OF TEXAS
HOMES FOR CHILDREN

8.

9.

10.

11.

12.

13.

14.

15.

ZOELLNER
ARTS
CENTER

LEHIGH University

1.

GULLIVER
BOOKS

2.

Gaslamp
SIXTH AVENUE

3.

4.

5.

6.

7.

8.

9.

10.

11.

12.

14.

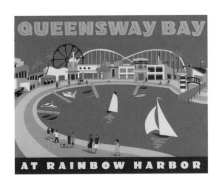

O C E A N P L A C E

13.

15.

1.

2.

3.

DANCEPORT RETAIL CENTRE
A RAMIREZ ENTERPRISE

4.

5.

INTELLISYS GROUP

6.

7.

(opposite)
Design Firm Dixon & Parcels Associates, Inc.

Client   Austin Quality Foods

1
Design Firm Cathey Associates, Inc.
2 - 4, 6 - 7
Design Firm The Dupuis Group
5
Design Firm Callery & Company

1. Client   The University Club
    Designers   Matt Westapher
                & Gordon Cathey

2. Client   Munchkin
    Designers   Bill Corridori, Jack Halpern,
                & Nobuko Komine

3. Client   Firehouse Subs
    Designer   John Silva

4. Client   Local Squeeze
    Designers   Steven DuPuis &
                Nobuko Komine

5. Client   Danceport
    Designer   Kelley Callery

6. Client   Van Kind Foods
    Designers   Bill Corridori, Nobuko Komine,
                & Jack Halpern

7. Client   Bausch & Lomb Surgical
    Designers   Bill Corridori & Jack Halpern

1.

MARINA
ACCESSORIES

2.

MONAGHAN
&COMPANY

BUILDING DOMINANT BRANDS

3.

BioMetrics™
SUPPLEMENT SYSTEMS

4.

Botanical
LABORATORIES

5.

PACIFIC CREST

6.

DCI·ENGINEERS
D'AMATO CONVERSANO INC.

7.

MARK KROESE

8.

Lagerlof
Bradley Senecal
& Swift LLP

RETELIGENT
C O R P O R A T I O N

9.

10.

THE **ENLORE**TECHNOLOGY GROUP

11.

CHINATOWN
INTERNATIONAL DISTRICT

12.

ON

14.

DACG FAST ED E

13.

15.

1 - 11
Design Firm Monaghan & Company
12 - 14
Design Firm Pentagram
15
Design Firm SBG Enterprise

1. Client   Marina Accessories, Inc.
   Designer   Tharon Knittle

2. Client   Monaghan & Company
   Designer   James Jahng

3. Client   Biometrics, Div. of
                      Land O Lakes
   Designer   Charlie Worcester

4. Client   Botanical Laboratories
   Designers   James Jahng
                      & Charlie Worcester

5. Client   Pacific Crest
   Designer   James Jahng

6. Client   DCI Engineers
   Designer   Charlie Worcester

7. Client   Adventure Media
   Designer   James Jahng

8. Client   Lagerlof/Senecal/Bradley
                      & Swift, LLP
   Designer   Dan Tagbo

9. Client   Reteligent Corporation
   Designers   James Jahng & Jon Greenbaum

10. Client   The Enlore Technology Group
    Designers James Jahng & Jon Greenbaum

11. Client   Chinatown Business Association
    Designer   James Jahng

12. Client   ON Semiconductor
    Designers Lowell Williams
                      & Wendy Carnegie

13. Client   TacoBueno
    Designers Lowell Williams, Woody Purtle,
                      & Leslie Purtle

14. Client   DACG
    Designers Lowell Williams &
                      Meggan Webber

15. Client   The Learning Company
    Designers Thomas Bond & Iraxte Mumford

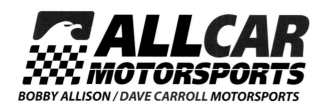

1.

2.

3.

4.

5.

6.

BLUE FIN CAFE & BILLIARDS

CANNERY ROW-MONTEREY, CA

7.

1 - 7
Design Firm The Wecker Group

1. Client   Allcar Motor Sports
    Designer   Robert Wecker

2. Client   Aqua Future, Inc.
    Designers   Robert Wecker & Matt Gnibus

3. Client   Aqua Future, Inc.
    Designers   Robert Wecker & Matt Gnibus

4. Client   Beeline Media Services
    Designer   Robert Wecker

5. Client   Blue Fin Billiards
    Designer   Robert Wecker

6. Client   Blue Fin Billiards
    Designer   Robert Wecker

7. Client   Universal Internet
    Designer   Robert Wecker

(opposite)
Design Firm Lister Butler Consulting

    Client   Horizon Blue Cross Blue Shield
                     of New Jersey
    Designer   William Davis

222

Horizon Blue Cross Blue Shield
of New Jersey

1.

2.

3.

4.

5.

6.

7.

8.

9.

10.

11.

12.

13.

14.

"Ariel"

15.

"Hawk"

1.

2.

3.

4.

5.

6.

7.
 **iChoose**

8.

9.

10.

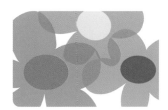

11.

12.

13.

Mary McMinn

14.

TECHNO-MATION

15.

1
Design Firm **Cathey Associates, Inc.**
2 - 15
Design Firm **Swieter Design**

1. Client   Media Research Corporation
              of America
   Designers Isabel Campos
              & Gordon Cathey

2. Client   Nextepp
   Designer Mark Ford

3. Client   Supre Inc.
   Designers Mark Waggoner
              & Carlos A. Perez

4. Client   Supre - Skin System
   Designer Erica Brinker

5. Client   Connectech
   Designer Mark Waggoner

6. Client   Bank Direct
   Designer Carlos A. Perez

7. Client   iChoose
   Designers Mark Waggoner, John Swieter,
              & Carlos A. Perez

8. Client   First Street
   Designers Ray Gallegos & Carlos A. Perez

9. Client   Techtonic
   Designer Carlos A. Perez

10. Client   T-Mech
    Designer Ray Gallegos

11. Client   Melissa Ronan
    Designer Mark Waggoner

12. Client   Inertia
    Designer Carlos A. Perez

13. Client   Dallas Heart Ball
    Designer Ray Gallegos

14. Client   Mary McMinn
    Designer Mark Waggoner

15. Client   Techno-Mation
    Designer Carlos A Perez

1.

2.

3.

4.

5.

6.

7.

GEAR UP FOR
SUMMER

(opposite)
Design Firm Sayles Graphic Design

Client   Muscular Dystrophy Association
              "Last Dinner on the Titanic"
Designer   John Sayles

1
Design Firm Lewis Design
2, 7
Design Firm Vitro Robertson
3
Design Firm Tyler Blik Design
4
Design Firm The Flowers Group
5
Design Firm Mires Design
6
Design Firm Maddocks & Co.

1. Client   Kidcare Express
   Designers   June Lewis & Tracy Sabin

2. Client   Rubio's Baja Grill
   Designers   Jeff Payne & Tracy Sabin

3. Client   Otay Ranch
   Designers   Ron Fleming & Tray Sabin

4. Client   The Ridge
   Designers   Cory Sheehan & Tracy Sabin

5. Client   Boy Scout Troop 260
   Designers   José Serrano & Tracy Sabin

6. Client   El Cholo
   Designers   Clare Sebenius & Tracy Sabin

7. Client   Shimano Resort
   Designers   John Bade & Tracy Sabin

1.

2.

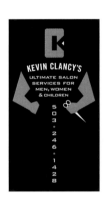

3.

4.

KEVIN CLANCY'S
ULTIMATE SALON
SERVICES FOR
MEN, WOMEN
& CHILDREN

503
•
246
•
1428

5.

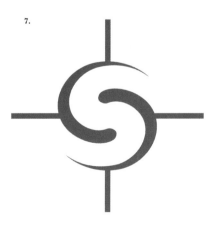

6.

RSR

RACE AND
SPORTSCAR
RESTORATION

7.

8.

DOTZERO

design

9.

10.

11.

12.

13.

14.

15.

(all)
Design Firm Dotzero Design

1. Client   Miller-Norris
   Designers   Jon Wippich & Karen Wippich

2. Client   Literacy Volunteers
   Designers   Jon Wippich & Karen Wippich

3. Client   HMH Advertising
      & Public Relatons
   Designer   Jon Wippich

4. Client   Kevin Clancy's
   Designers   Jon Wippich & Karen Wippich

5. Client   Underground Storage
   Designers   Karen Wippich & Jon Wippich

6. Client   RSR

7. Client   Standard Printing
   Designers   Jon Wippich & Karen Wippich

8. Client   Dotzero Design
   Designers   Karen Wippich & Jon Wippich

9. Client   Classique Images
   Designers   Karen Wippich & Jon Wippich

10. Client   The Bodo Ensemble
    Designers   Karen Wippich & Jon Wippich

11. Client   Mostella Records
    Designers   Jon Wippich & Karen Wippich

12. Client   Planet Salon
    Designers   Karen Wippich & Jon Wippich

13. Client   Star Advisors
    Designers   Jon Wippich & Karen Wippich

14. Client   HMH Adv./Louisiana-Pacific
    Designer   Jon Wippich

15. Client   Jodie Day
    Designers   Karen Wippich & Jon Wippich

1.

DOGLOO ®

2.

**Big Sisters
of Los Angeles**

3.

creative
solutions
group

4.

Black & Blu
E N T E R T A I N M E N T

5.

6.

C\|||C

7.

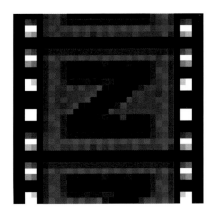

1 - 7
Design Firm Zamboo

1. Client   Dogloo
   Designer   Dave Zambotti

2. Client   Big Sisters of LA
   Designer   Dave Zambotti

3. Client   Creative Solutions Group
   Designer   Becca Bootes

4. Client   Black & Blu
   Designers   Dave Zambotti & Jeff Allison

5. Client   Premiere Dental
   Designers   Dave Zambotti & Becca Bootes

6. Client   CMC
   Designers   Becca Bootes & Dave Zambotti

7. Client   Zfilmmaker
   Designer   Dave Zambotti

(opposite)
Design Firm Sabingrafik, Inc.

   Client   Odyssey
   Designers   Lisa Peters & Tracy Sabin

ODYSSEY

1.

2.

3.

4.

5.

6.

7.

8.

9.

10.

11.

12.

13.

14.

SIGNATURE
PLASTIC SURGERY

15.

1 - 6, 8 - 9
Design Firm Zamboo
7, 11
Design Firm Cathey Associates, Inc.
10, 12 - 14
Design Firm Lotas Minard Patton McIver
15
Design Firm Dixon & Parcels Associates, Inc.

1. Client   ORBA
   Designer   Becca Bootes

2. Client   Pharos Optics
   Designer   Becca Bootes

3. Client   Baton Records
   Designer   Dave Zambotti

4. Client   Windy City Productions
   Designer   Becca Bootes

5. Client   Demand
   Designers   Dave Zambotti, Chris Go,
                & Becca Bootes

6. Client   Tops
   Designer   Dave Zambotti

7. Client   Ultimate Race Vacations
   Designer   Gordon Cathey

8. Client   Solsource
   Designers   Becca Bootes, Chris Go,
                & Dave Zambotti

9. Client   Doggone Gourmet
   Designers   Dave Zambotti & Chris Sharp

10. Client   Dana (Shades)
    Designers   Kristin Moore-Gantz
                & Suzan Merritt

11. Client   Center for Housing Resources
    Designer   Gordon Cathey

12. Client   Nutratech Inc
    Designer   Daniela Ganem

13. Client   Landon Media Group
    Designer   Yucel Erdogan

14. Client   Signature Plastic Surgery
    Designer   Yucel Erdogan

15. Client   Austin Quality Foods, Inc.

1.

2.

3.

4.

5.

6.

7.

8.

236

9.

10.

11.

12.

13.

14.

15.

FRESH-CAUGHT TASTE!

15.

1 - 9
Design Firm Hans Flink Design Inc.
10 - 14
Design Firm Sayles Graphic Design
15
Design Firm Faine-Oller Productions, Inc.

1.	Client	Colgate-Palmolive (Speed Stick)
	Designers	Mark Krukonis
		& Susan Kunschaft
2.	Client	Unilever HPC, USA
		(Mentadent)
	Designer	Chang-Mei Lin
3.	Client	Whitehall-Robins
		(Centrum Performance)
	Designers	Chang-Mei Lin
		& Susan Kunschaft
4.	Client	Unilever HPC, USA (Sunlight)
	Designers	Michael Troian
		& Harry Bertschmann
5.	Client	Unilever HPC, USA
		(Crystal Ice)
	Designers	Susan Kunschaft
		& Chang-Mi Lin
6.	Client	Serenity Garden & Home
	Designers	Loi Van Name & Hans D. Flink

7.	Client	Unilever HPC, USA
		(Pond's Clear Solutions)
	Designers	Chang Mei-Lin, Susan
		Kunschaft, & Michael Troian
8.	Client	Pfizer Inc. (Bengay SPA)
	Designer	Chang-Mei Lin
9.	Client	Mead Johnson (Alacta)
	Designer	Susan Kunschaft
10.	Client	Starr Litigation Services, Inc.
	Designer	John Sayles
11.	Client	Barrick Roofing
	Designer	John Sayles
12.	Client	Casa Bonita
	Designer	John Sayles
13.	Client	Glazed Expressions
	Designer	John Sayles
14.	Client	Pattee Enterprises
	Designer	John Sayles
15.	Client	Coleson Foods, Inc.
	Designers	Catherine Oller, Barbara Faine,
		Bruce Hale, & Steve Coppin

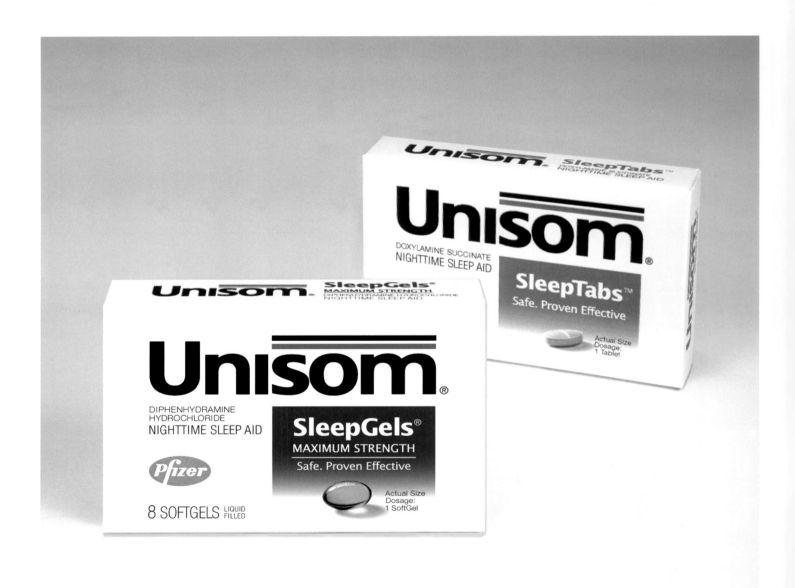

1.

2.

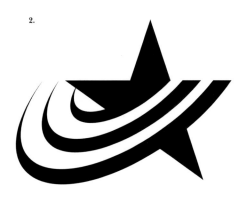

3.

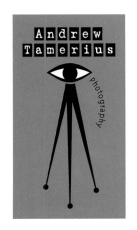

4.

5.

6.

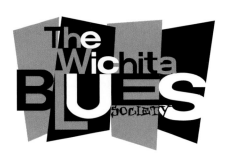

7.

(opposite)
Design Firm   Hans Flink Design Inc.

Client   Pfizer Inc. (Unisom)
Designers   Michael Troian
               & Harry Berschmann

1 - 7
Design Firm   Dotzero Design

1. Client   Star Advisors Softball Team
   Designers   Jon Wippich & Karen Wippich

2. Client   Star Advisors Program Logo
   Designers   Karen Wippich & Jon Wippich

3. Client   Star Advisors Night Flight Event
   Designers   Jon Wippich & Karen Wippich

4. Client   HMH Advertising/
               Louisiana-Pacific
   Designer   Jon Wippich

5. Client   The Wichita Blues Society,
               Blues Brunch
   Designers   Karen Wippich & Jon Wippich

6. Client   Wichita Blues Society
   Designers   Karen Wippich & Jon Wippich

7. Client   Andrew Tamerius Photography
   Designers   Karen Wippich & Jon Wippich

1.

2.

Integrated Concepts
INCORPORATED

3.

FIFTH 5 FLOOR
PRODUCTION MUSIC LIBRARY

4.

5.

6.

7.

8.

9.

10.

11.

12.

13.

14.

**CARMEL MARINA
CORPORATION**

15.

1 - 5
Design Firm   Innovative Design & Advertising
6 - 11, 13 - 15
Design Firm   The Wecker Group
12
Design Firm   Maxi Harper Graphics

1. Client   Markie D's Restaurant
   Designers   Kim Crossett-Neumann
                & Susan Nickey-Newton

2. Client   ITM
   Designers   Kim Crossett-Neumann
                & Susan Nickey-Newton

3. Client   ABC-5th Floor Production
                Music Library
   Designers   Kim Crossett-Neumann
                & Susan Nickey-Newton

4. Client   vico
   Designers   Kim Crossett-Neumann
                & Susan Nickey-Newton

5. Client   Adamm's Stained Glass
   Designers   Kim Crossett-Neumann, Susan
                Nickey-Newton, & Dan Cotton

6. Client   Café au Lait Restaurant
   Designers   Robert Wecker

7. Client   California Insurance Group
   Designer   Robert Wecker

8. Client   California
                Restaurant Association
   Designer   Robert Wecker

9. Client   Caruso's Corner
   Designer   Robert Wecker

10. Client   Cypress Tree Inn
    Designer   Robert Wecker

11. Client   Cannery Row Inn
    Designer   Robert Wecker
    Illustrator Mark Savee

12. Client   Terlingua
    Designer   Maxi Harper

13. Client   Carmel Area Waste
                Management District
    Designer   Robert Wecker

14. Client   Carmel Marina Corporation
    Designer   Robert Wecker

15. Client   Carmel Valley Inn &
                Tennis Resort
    Designer   Robert Wecker

1.

2.

Brookfield Zoo

3.

4.

5.

6.

7.

1
 Design Firm Wizards/Spire Design
2 - 4
 Design Firm Brookfield Zoo
5, 7
 Design Firm Squires & Company
6
 Designer   Brandon Murphy

1. Client   Wizards of the Coast

2, 3
   Client   Brookfield Zoo
   Designer   Hannah Jennings
   Illustrator   Edith Emmengger

4. Client   Brookfield Zoo
   Designers   Andrew Murashige &
                   Peter Skach
   Illustrator   Jeff O'Connor

5. Client   Techware Information Systems
   Designer   Anna Magruder

6. Client   Motion Projects
   Designer   Brandon Murphy

7. Client   Bill Jackson Associates
   Designer   Christie Grotheim

(opposite)
   Design Firm Sayles Graphic Design

8. Client   1999 Iowa State Fair
                   "Knock Yourself Out"
   Designer   John Sayles

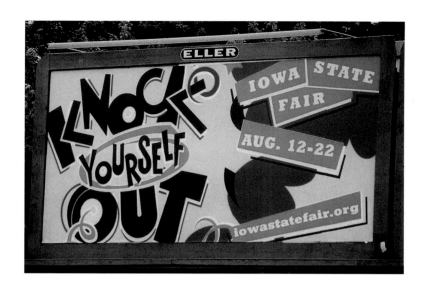

1.

2.

3.

4.

5.

6.

7.

8.

9.

10.

11.

12.

FRIENDS OF
CALIFORNIA STATE
UNIVERSITY
MONTEREY BAY

13.

14.

15.

1.

2.

3.

4.

5.

6.

7.

8.

9.

10.

11.

12.

PHILADELPHIA
registered nurse
practitioner

13.

14.

15.

1 - 13
Design Firm   Georgopulos Design
14, 15
Design Firm   Misha Design Studio

1. Client   Georgopulos Design
    Designer   Jonathan Georgopulos

2. Client   Red Hand Records
    Designer   Jonathan Georgopulos

3. Client   SunGard
    Designer   Jonathan Georgopulos

4. Client   N
    Designer   Jonathan Georgopulos

5. Client   Arts Fest 2000
    Designer   Jonathan Georgopulos

6. Client   SunGard
    Designer   Jonathan Georgopulos

7. Client   Neon
    Designer   Jonathan Georgopulos

8. Client   SunGard
    Designer   Jonathan Georgopulos

9. Client   Global Plus
    Designer   Jonathan Georgopulos

10, 11
    Client   SunGard
    Designer   Jonathan Georgopulos

12. Client   econsortium
    Designer   Jonathan Georgopulos

13. Client   PHL Nurse Association
    Designer   Jonathan Georgopulos

14. Client   Brookline Dental Studio
    Designer   Misha Lenn

15. Client   Boston Ballet
    Designer   Misha Lenn

1.

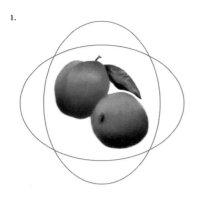

2.

3.

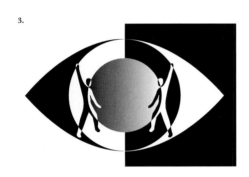

4.

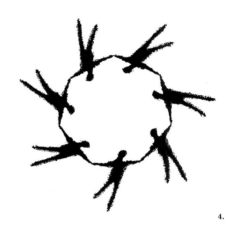

5.

6.

7.

(opposite)
Design Firm Kollberg/Johnson

Client   Snowball Foods
Designers   Kollberg/Johnson

1 - 6
Design Firm Rockmorris Design
7
Design Firm Callery & Company

1. Client   Peach^2
    Designer   Rock Morris

2. Client   Olympic Sea & Sky
    Designer   Rock Morris

3. Client   Vis•Tech
    Designer   Rock Morris

4. Client   Inhaus Strategies
    Designer   Rock Morris

5. Client   F.C. Jr. Transport
    Designer   Rock Morris

6. Client   Gators'
    Designer   Rock Morris

7. Client   Flexographic Tech Assoc.
    Designer   Kelley Callery

1.

2.

Rehabilitation Providers

3.

Running Iron

RESTAURANT AND SALOON

4.

5.

6.

7.

8.

250

9.

MONTEREY SPORTS CENTER

SUNSET TENNIS CLASSIC

10.

MONTEREY PENINSULA CHAMBER OF COMMERCE

11.

LIST ENGINEERING COMPANY

Mechanical Consultants

12.

SOQUEL CREEK WATER DISTRICT

13.

San Juan Bautista
Chamber of Commerce

14.

PELICAN PIZZA

15.

1 - 15
Design Firm   The Wecker Group

1, 2	Client	Laguna Seca Raceway		9.	Client	Monterey Sports Center
	Designer	Robert Wecker			Designer	Robert Wecker
3.	Client	Rehabilitation Providers		10.	Client	Pacific Grove Rotary Club
	Designer	Robert Wecker			Designer	Robert Wecker
4.	Client	Running Iron Restaurant		11.	Client	Monterey Peninsula
	Designer	Robert Wecker				Chamber of Commerce
	Illustrator	Mark Savee			Designer	Robert Wecker
5.	Client	Monterey.com, Inc.		12.	Client	List Engineering Company
	Designer	Robert Wecker			Designer	Robert Wecker
6.	Client	Ryan Ranch Rotisserie		13.	Client	Soquel Creek Water District
	Designer	Robert Wecker			Designer	Robert Wecker
7.	Client	Red's Donuts		14.	Client	San Juan Bautista
	Designer	Robert Wecker				Chamber of Commerce
	Illustrator	Mark Savee			Designer	Robert Wecker
8.	Client	The Hearth Shop		15.	Client	Pelican Pizza
	Designer	Robert Wecker			Designer	Robert Wecker

1.

2.

3.

4.

5.

6.

7.

1 - 2
Design Firm Maxi Harper Graphics
3 - 7
Design Firm Gable Design Group

1. Client   Marhatis: Spiritual-Healer
               of Three Goddesses
   Designer   Maxi Harper

2. Client   SPT
   Designer   Maxi Harper

3. Client   Kenny G
   Designer   Damon Nakagawa

4. Client   cobid.net
   Designer   Damon Nakagawa

5. Client   Glenn Sound
   Designers   Damon Nakagawa
                & Ayumi Inoue

6. Client   Art Turock & Associates
   Designers   Tony Gable & Damon Nakagawa

7. Client   City of Seattle
   Designers   Tony Gable & Damon Nakagawa

(opposite)
Design Firm DYNAPAC Design Group

   Client   Harbor Lights Candle Shop
   Designer   Lee A. Aellig

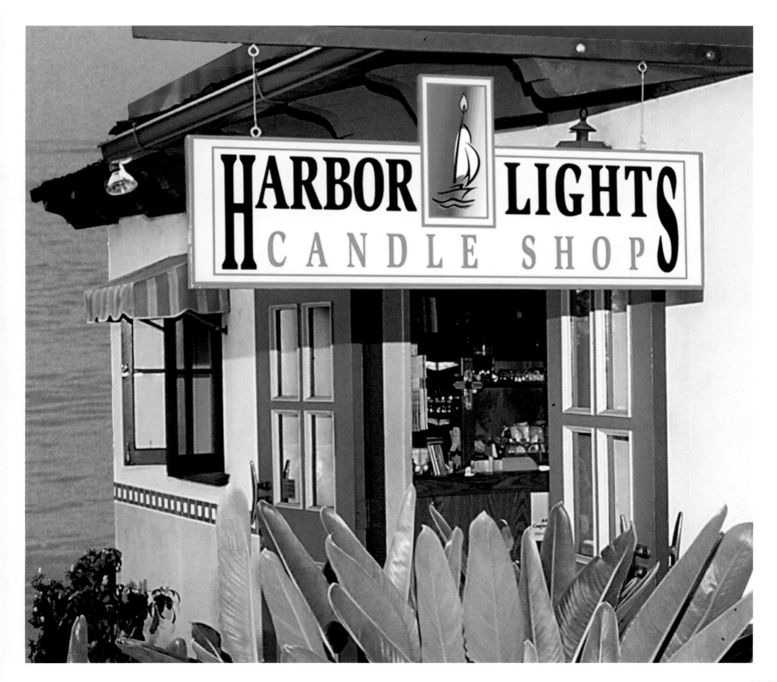

Rubbish

1.

2.

3.

4.

APPLIANT

5.

jacknabbit.com

6.

Lingo

7.

8.

254

9.

10.

11.

12.

HealingMD™

13.

The Leisure Company

14.

15.

1 - 10
Design Firm David Lemley Design
11 - 13
Design Firm 30sixty design inc.
14
Design Firm Deutsch Design Works
15
Design Firm Greenfield/Belser Ltd.

1. Client   Nordstrom
   Designer   David Lemley

2. Client   David Lemley Design
   Designer   David Lemley

3. Client   The Bon Marché
   Designer   David Lemley

4. Client   Bald Beaver Brewing Company
   Designers   David Lemley & Matt Peloza

5. Client   Appliant, Inc.
   Designer   David Lemley

6. Client   jacknabbit.com
   Designers   David Lemley & Emma Wilson

7. Client   Active Voice
   Designer   David Lemley

8. Client   One Reel/Bumbershoot
   Designer   David Lemley

9. Client   David Lemley Design
   Designer   David Lemley

10. Client   One Reel/Bumbershoot
    Designer   David Lemley

11. Client   30sixty design airways
    Designer   Pär Larsson

12. Client   Club 30/60
    Designer   Pär Larsson

13. Client   Healing MD
    Designer   Christine Jaskowiak

14. Client   American West Airlines
    Designers   Barry Deutsch &
                 Jess Giambroni

15. Client   Weinberg Group
    Designers   Burkey Belser & Tom Cameron

distilled images

a picture's worth

1.

2.

TRiBE

[moving]

Pictures

3.

4.

in2books

A Reading Pen Pal Program

™

5.

6.

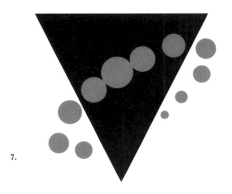

7.

8.

256

9.
© Pen 1, 1997

10.

11.

12.

13.

14.

15.

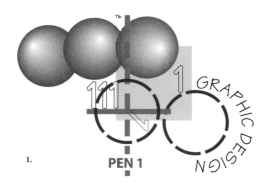

1.

PEN 1

PHILLIBER
RESEARCH
ASSOCIATES

2.

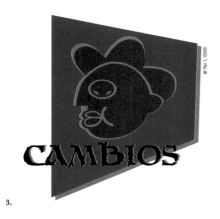

CAMBIOS

3.

TEEN OUTREACH PROGRAM

4.

TEEN OUTREACH PROGRAM

21st CENTURY COMMUNITY CENTERS
LEARNING

5.

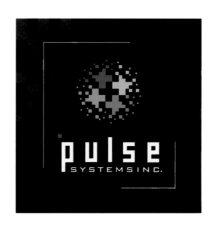

pulse
SYSTEMS INC.

6.

Fran's
CHOCOLATES, LTD.

7.

(opposite)
Design Firm **Insight Design Communications**

Client   Richard Lynn's Shoe Market
Designers   Sherrie & Tracy Holdeman

1 - 5
Design Firm **Pen 1**

6
Design Firm **Insight Design Communications**

7
Design Firm **Walsh & Associates, Inc.**

1. Client   Pen 1
    Designer   Karen Bahadori

2. Client   Philliber Research Associates
    Designer   Karen Bahadori

3. Client   Teen Outreach Program/
                     Cambios
    Designers   Karen Bahadori &
                     Alicia Colina-Ashby

4, 5
    Client   Teen Outreach Program
    Designer   Karen Bahadori

6. Client   Pulse System Inc.
    Designers   Sherrie & Tracy Holdeman

7. Client   Fran's Chocolates Ltd.
    Designer   Miriam Lisco

1.

2.

3.

4.

5.

PPI Entertainment

6.

7.

AKADÉMOS.COM

8.

9.

SHIMIZU DESIGN STUDIO INC.

10.

11.

Harvest Moon ™

The best meals under the moon.

12.

13.

ASSASSINS

14.

15.

1 - 5
  Design Firm A+B (In Exile)
6 - 9
  Design Firm Iron Design
10
  Design Firm Shimizu Design Studio, Inc.
11 - 12
  Design Firm Adkins/Balchunas
13
  Design Firm Dever Designs
14
  Design Firm Rickabaugh Graphics
15
  Design Firm Fine Design Group

1. Client "S"-Team, Ljubljana

2. Client "Heart of the City"
  Designer Eduard Cehovin

3. Client National Examination Center
  (Slovenia)/East Meet West
  Designer Eduard Cehovin

4. Client Telekom-Srbija

5. Client "A Atalanta"
  Designer Eduard Cehovin

6. Client Peter Pan Industries
  Designer Ted Skibinski

7. Client Pandee Games
  Designer Todd Edmonds

8. Client Akademos.com
  Designer Ted Skibinski

9. Client Imode Retrieval Systems
  Designer Todd Edmonds

10. Client Shimizu Design Studio, Inc.
  Designers Ichiro Shimizu &
  Hiroto Takahashi

11. Client London Lennies
  Designers Jerry Balchunas
  & Susan DeAngelis

12. Client Harvest Moon
  Designers Jerry Balchunas
  & Susan DeAngelis

13. Client Center for Population
  Health and Nutrition
  Designer Jeffrey L. Dever

14. Client Players Theatre
  Designer Eric Rickabaugh

15. Client Western Exhibitors, Inc.
  Designers Jake Barlow, John Taylor,
  & Kenn Fine

1.

2.

3.

4.

5.

6.

7.

(all)

Design Firm Insight Design Communications

1. Client   gardenandholiday.com
    Designers   Sherrie and Tracy Holdeman

2. Client   eMeter
    Designers   Sherrie and Tracy Holdeman

3, 4
    Client   The Hayes Co.
    Designers   Sherrie and Tracy Holdeman

5. Client   Howard's Optique
    Designers   Sherrie and Tracy Holdeman

6. Client   Physique Enhancement
    Designers   Sherrie and Tracy Holdeman

7. Client   Gear Up
    Designers   Sherrie and Tracy Holdeman

(opposite)
Design Firm Whitney Stinger, Inc.

    Client   Bone Daddy +
                  The Blues Shakers
    Designers   Mike Whitney & Karl Stinger

d'MUIR

1.

Axua

2.

e m f
EVAPORATED METAL FILMS

3.

4.

im○de

retrievalsystems

5.

6.

312

CollegeAvenue

7.

SMARTCARD
TECHNOLOGY
CENTER

8

The Replication Challenge:

Lessons Learned from the

National Replication Project for
the Teen Outreach Program (TOP)

The Replication Challenge: Lessons Learned from the National Replication Project for the Teen Outreach Program (TOP)

9.

10.

11.

12.

14.

WIRELESS SHOWCASE ASIA

13.

HOLY

TRINITY

CATHOLIC

CHURCH

1787 ANNO DOMINI

15.

1 - 7			
Design Firm	**Iron Design**		
8, 10 - 14			
Design Firm	**Tim Kenney Design Partners**		
9			
Design Firm	**Pen 1**		
15			
Design Firm	**Lawson Design**		

1. Client	Marietta Corp.	
Designer	Todd Edmonds	
2. Client	AXUA	
Designer	Todd Edmonds	
3. Client	Evaporated Metal Films Corp.	
Designer	Todd Edmonds	
4. Client	Momentum Media	
Designer	Jim Keller	
5. Client	Imode Retrieval Systems	
Designer	Todd Edmonds	
6. Client	Rip Cord Games	
Designer	Jim Keller	
7. Client	Integrated Acquisitions & Development	
Designer	Todd Edmonds	

8. Client	GSA (General Services Administration)
Designer	Tim Kenney
9. Client	Teen Outreach Program
Designer	Karen Bahadori
10. Client	Compliance Inc.
Designer	Tim Kenney
11. Client	Sigma-Tau Pharmaceuticals, Inc. (proXeed)
Designer	Tim Kenney
12. Client	New Dominion Resources Corporation (x-tabs)
Designer	Monica Banko
13. Client	PCIA (Personal Communications Industry Association)
Designer	Charlene Gamba
14. Client	Holy Trinity Catholic Church
Designer	Tim Kenney
15. Client	Rubin Postaer & Assoc. (Acura)
Designers	Jeff Lawson & Bob Francis

LAMSON, DUGAN & MURRAY

1.

The Club for Kids with Asthma

2.

3.

Scott Hamilton
**Circle *of* Friends
Invitational**

4.

Woodwinds
Health Campus

5.

**Science
Museum**
of Minnesota

6.

net radio .com

7.

PAZZALUNA
URBAN TRATTORIA & BAR

8.

fraîche
a fresh concept in cosmetics

9.

ULM
HOLDING CORPORATION COMMERCIAL REAL ESTATE
1776 BROADWAY ▪ SUITE 2000 ▪ NEW YORK, NY 10019

10.

11.

TRĒO®

12.

BEST BUYER'S BROKER REALTY INC.

13.

KELME

14.

KELME

15.

1, 2
Design Firm Dotzler Creative Arts
3
Design Firm Curry Design Associates
4 - 8
Design Firm Little & Company
9 - 13
Design Firm Hirschhorn & Young Inc.
14, 15
Design Firm Lawson Design

1. Client   Lamson, Dugan & Murray

2. Client   AsthmaBusters

3. Client   Muse X Editions
    Designer   Steve Curry

4. Client   Scott Hamilton Circle of Friends
    Designers   Monica Little, Jim Jackson,
                  Mike Schacherer, & Viet Do

5. Client   Woodwinds Health Campus
    Designers   Monica Little, Jim Jackson,
                  Scott Sorenson, & Viet Do

6. Client   Science Museum of Minnesota
    Designers   Monica Little, Jim Jackson,
                  & Michael Lizama

7. Client   Netradio.com
    Designers   Monica Little, Stefan Hartung,
                  & Scott Sorenson

8. Client   Morissey Hospitality—
                  Pazzaluna Restaurant
    Designers   Monica Little, Jim Jackson,
                  Michael Lizama, & Viet Do

9. Client   Urban Retreat Day Spa
    Designer   Barbara Reed

10. Client   ULM Holding Corporation
    Designer   Barbara Reed

11. Client   The Lion Construction
                  Group Inc.
    Designer   Barbara Reed

12. Client   Primavera Laboratories, Inc.
    Designer   Barbara Reed

13. Client   Best Buyer's Broker Realty
    Designer   Barbara Reed

14, 15
    Client   Concept 21 (Kelme Shoes)
    Designers   Jeff Lawson & Brent James

Whitney Stinger

EVD Advertising

A Taste of Arlington

Enterworks ℠

powerize.com

neonatal
STRATEGIC PARTNERSHIP

CORE
SOFTWARE

V A N S C O Y ∞

1.

2.

3.

4.

6.

5.

7.

(opposite)
Design Firm Whitney Stinger

Client   Whitney Stinger, Inc
Designers   Mike Whitney & Karl Stinger

1 - 5
Design Firm EVD Advertising
6, 7
Design Firm Curry Design Associates

1. Client   EVD Advertising
   Designers   Rachel Deutsch & David Street

2. Client   Taste of Arlington
   Designers   Rachel Deutsch & Marc Foelsch

3. Client   Enterworks
   Designers   Rachel Deutsch, Blake Stenning,
                    & Marc Foelsch

4. Client   Powerize
   Designers   Rachel Deutsch &
                    Tom Cosgrove

5. Client   Neonatal Strategic Partnership
   Designers   Rachel Deutsch & Marc Foelsch

6. Client   Core Software Technology
   Designer   Jason Scheideman

7. Client   VanScoy Photography
   Designer   Jason Scheideman

1.

2.

3.

4.

5.

6.

7.

8.

WINGATE
UNIVERSITY

9.

10.

11.

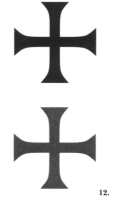

12.

13.

14.

15.

1 - 8
Design Firm Iconixx
              (Iconixx Web Development)

9 - 14
Design Firm Steve Thomas
              Marketing Communications

15
Design Firm EVD Advertising

1. Client   The Mark Winkler Company
    Designers   Gretchen Frederick &
                   Anjeanette Agro

2. Client   Aspire Technology Group
    Designers   John Cabot Lodge &
                   Robin Clay Diamond

3. Client   Riggs Bank NA
    Designers   John Cabot Lodge &
                   Andrew Johnson
    Illustrator   Mark Summers

4. Client   Neu Star, Inc.
    Designers   John Cabot Lodge &
                   Lara Santos

5. Client   FBR.com
    Designer   Andrew Johnson

6. Client   Pace Financial Network, LLC
    Designers   John Cabot Lodge &
                   Lara Santos

7. Client   Redbricks.com
    Designers   John Cabot Lodge &
                   Lara Santos

8. Client   Madison Asset Marketplace
    Designers   John Cabot Lodge, Mary
                   Parsons, & Chuck Sundin

9. Client   Wingate University
    Designer   Steve Thomas

10. Client   UNC Charlotte
    Designer   Steve Thomas

11. Client   Mississippi Valley State
                   University
    Designer   Steve Thomas

12. Client   Church of the Beloved
    Designer   Steve Thomas

13. Client   Charlotte Country Day School
    Designers   Steve Thomas & Dan Wold

14. Client   American Security Mortgage
    Designer   Steve Thomas

15. Client   Riverbed Technologies
    Designers   Rachel Deutsch &
                   Marc Foelsch

1.

2.

3.

4.

5.

6.

7.

1
Design Firm **California Design International**
2 - 7
Design Firm **Dotzler Creative Arts**

1. Client   Diamond Lane Communication
   Designers Linda Kelley & Dan Liew

2. Client   Step Up To Life

3. Client   Christ For The City

4. Client   Accu-Cut

5. Client   Hope Center

6. Client   KGBI

7. Client   Trinity Church

(opposite)
Design Firm **Templin Brink Design**

   Client   Classic Company
   Designer Joel Templin

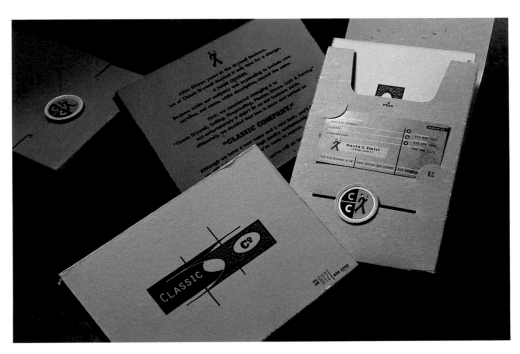

TRUEVISION

1.

TRUEVISION
FOUNDATION

2.

formfunction

3.

4.

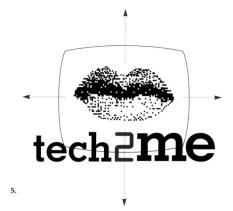

tech2me

5.

SOUTHWEST
TIRE & AUTO
GENERAL

6.

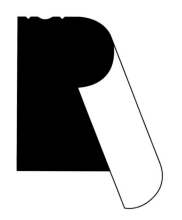

7.

SAGE

8.

the dancing chef

9.

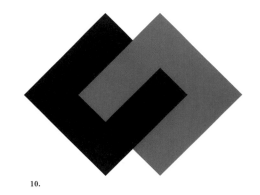

10.

T H E
A R T
I C H
O K E
C A F E

11.

RAA

12.

NATIONAL
ATOMIC
MUSEUM

13.

Portobello

14.

CLIF SHOT®

15.

1 - 14		
Design Firm	**Studio Hill Design**	
15		
Design Firm	**California Design International**	

1, 2		
Client	TrueVision International	
Designer	Sandy Hill	

3, 4		
Client	Form + Function	
Designers	Sandy Hill & Emma Roberts	

5.	Client	Tech2Me
	Designers	Sandy Hill & Emma Roberts

6.	Client	Southwest General Tire
	Designers	Sandy Hill & Emma Roberts

7.	Client	Robert Reck Photography
	Designers	Sandy Hill & Emma Roberts

8.	Client	Sage
	Designers	Sandy Hill & Emma Roberts

9.	Client	Dancing Chef
	Designer	Sandy Hill

10.	Client	Christy Construction
	Designer	Sandy Hill

11.	Client	Artichoke Cafe
	Designers	Sandy Hill & Emma Roberts

12.	Client	Radiology Associates
	Designers	Sandy Hill & Emma Roberts

13.	Client	National Atomic Museum
	Designers	Sandy Hill, Alan Shimato, & Mary Lambert

14.	Client	Portobello Restaurant
	Designers	Sandy Hill & Emma Roberts

15.	Client	Clif Shot
	Designers	Linda Kelley & Suzy Leung

1.

Vantis' Complete Programmable Logic Software Solution

2.

T·P·R

3.

Real Estate Energy Solutions

SM

4.

PENSARE™

5.

6.

7.

8.

9.

MOAI
TECHNOLOGIES

10.

11.

INKTOMI

12.

education
connect

13.

GALIL
WE MOVE THE WORLD

14.

15.

1.

2.

3.

4.

5.

World*Blaze*

6.

7.

(opposite)
Design Firm Foote, Cone, & Belding

Client   Levi Strauss & Co.
Designer   Joel Templin

1 - 5
Design Firm Gunion Design
6, 7
Design Firm California Design International

1. Client   Sakura of America
    Designer   Jefrey Gunion

2. Client   Dolphin Ventures
    Designer   Jefrey Gunion

3. Client   Codår Ocean Sensors
    Designer   Jefrey Gunion

4. Client   Life Action Partnership, Inc.
    Designer   Jefrey Gunion

5. Client   Apex Adventures
    Designer   Jefrey Gunion

6. Client   World Blaize
    Designers   Linda Kelley & Dan Liew

7. Client   Vivant!
    Designers   Linda Kelley & Brian Sasville

1.

2.

RED   LINE   Levi's

3.

4.

ACTION
marketing group

5.

6.

7.

8.

9.

10.

11.

12.

13.

Divorced Fathers
Network

14.

15.

1, 2, 4 - 8
Design Firm Templin Brink Design
3
Design Firm Foote, Cone, & Belding
9 - 11
Design Firm Angela Jackson Design
12 - 15
Design Firm Gunion Design

1. Client   Sparks.com
   Designer   Joel Templin

2. Client   Jon Gipe Photo
   Designer   Joel Templin

3. Client   Levi Strauss & Co.
   Designer   Joel Templin

4. Client   Spinner.com
   Designers   Gaby Brink & Paul Howalt

5. Client   Action Marketing Group
   Designers   Joel Templin & Gaby Brink

6. Client   idream.com
   Designer   Joel Templin

7. Client   Cobaltcard.com
   Designers   Joel Templin & Paul Howalt

8. Client   Yodlee.com
   Designers   Joel Templin & Paul Howalt

9. Client   Friends of Auburn/Tahoe Vista
                 Placer County Animal Shelter
   Designers   Angela Jackson &
                 Nina Courtney

10. Client   Angela Jackson
    Designer   Angela Jackson

11. Client   Rosemary Friborn
    Designer   Angela Jackson

12. Client   Gunion Design
    Designer   Jefrey Gunion

13. Client   Shear Edge
    Designer   Jefrey Gunion

14. Client   Divorced Fathers Network
    Designer   Jefrey Gunion

15. Client   PGW Websites
    Designer   Jefrey Gunion

TOMORROW FACTORY

1.

2.

phoenix>pop

3.

AMAZ○N.COM

4.

CUT FROM THE ORIGINAL CLOTH™

DOCKERS® **K-1** KHAKIS

1932 Combat Army Cloth Adopted, U.S. Army.

5.

Designed by
SOUTHPARK FABRICATORS | San Francisco, CA
tel | 415-897-6622

6.

WineShopper.COM

7.

1 - 7

Design Firm Templin Brink Design

1. Client   Tomorrow Factory
    Designer   Joel Templin

2. Client   Warren Miller
    Designers   Joel Templin, Paul Howalt,
                 & Gaby Brink

3. Client   Phoenix- Pop
    Designer   Joel Templin

4. Client   Amazon.com
    Designer   Joel Templin

5. Client   Dockers Khakis
    Designer   Gaby Brink

6. Client   Southpark Fabricators
    Designer   Gaby Brink

7. Client   WineShopper.com
    Designers   Gaby Brink & Joel Templin

(opposite)
**Design Firm Insight Design
             Communications**

Client   With A Twist
Designers   Sherrie Holdeman
              & Tracy Holdeman

WITH A TWIST

foodandgifts.com

1.

2.

THE

KINDERPLATZ

OF FINE ARTS

CUISINE
CELLARS

3.

AGRIAMERICA

4.

AMERICA'S FINEST

TRI ★ VALLEY™

GROWERS

5.

KAUAI
COFFEE
I Wahi Kope Nāu?

6.

CollegeEdge

7.

8.

Lucille & Henry
Home Textiles

9.

DESTINATION EUROPE
LIMITED

10.

SANTANA ROW

11.

MAX

12.

Gardenburger

14.

DESTINATION
HOTELS & RESORTS

13.

confer
The Leader in Care Chain Management™

15.

1.

BALLENTINE
D E S I G N S

2.

3.

4.

5.

6.

7.

8.

MEADOWBANK ESTATES

9.

10.

SJ Corio Company

AUCTIONS   APPRAISALS   LIQUIDATIONS

11.

BAYOU

CARDIOTHORACIC

SURGERY ASSOCIATES, LTD

12.

Blue Sky

SPA WORKS

13.

14.

Pivot

MARKETING DATA

SERVICES, LLC.

15.

1 - 5
Design Firm   Monica Reskala
6 - 15
Design Firm   Creative Vision Design Co.

1. Client   Ballentine Designs
    Designer   Monica Reskala

2. Client   Bridge Film
    Designer   Monica Reskala

3. Client   Europa Espresso Bars
    Designer   Monica Reskala

4, 5
    Client   Zeum
    Designer   Monica Reskala

6. Client   S.J. Corio, Company
    Designer   Greg Gonsalves

7. Client   Native, Inc.
    Designer   Greg Gonsalves

8. Client   PastaWorks
    Designer   Greg Gonsalves

9. Client   Empson U.S.A.
    Designer   Greg Gonsalves

10. Client   Coffee Fields
    Designer   Greg Gonsalves

11. Client   S.J. Corio Company
    Designer   Greg Gonsalves

12. Client   Bayou C.S.A.
    Designer   Greg Gonsalves

13. Client   Blue Sky Spaworks
    Designer   Greg Gonsalves

14. Client   Image By Design
    Designer   Greg Gonsalves

15. Client   Pivot, LLC.
    Designer   Greg Gonsalves

1.

2.

T H E
CENTRAL EXCHANGE
3.

4.

Alegria
W I N E R Y
5.

SCHELLING
6.

SCOTT'S
S E A F O O D
7.

Kristen
Anacker
COSTUME DESIGN & PRODUCTION
8.

9.

1.

2.

3.

4.

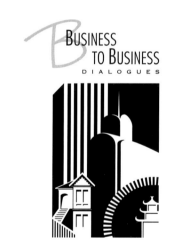

5.

6.

7.

8.

9.

10.

11.

12.

13.

14.

CHASE FUNDS

15.

1 - 10
    Design Firm **McKenzie & Associates, Inc.**
11, 12, 14, 15
    Design Firm **Hanson Associates, Inc.**
13
    Design Firm **Studio Morris**

1. Client   The Golden Gate
               Game Company
    Designers   Jean McKenzie &
               Misho Stawnecky

2. Client   Pacific Pet Service
    Designers   Jean McKenzie &
               Misho Stawnecky

3. Client   Ernst & Young
    Designers   Jean McKenzie, Shannon
               Sanders, & Brad Walton

4. Client   Ernst & Young
    Designers   Jean McKenzie & Jonina Skaggs

5. Client   The City of Hope
    Designers   Jean McKenzie, Debbie Murzyn,
               & Shannon Sanders

6. Client   Ernst & Young
    Designers   Jean McKenzie, Debbie Murzyn,
               & Daniel McClain

7. Client   CSS, Complete Software
               Solutions
    Designers   Jean McKenzie & Debbi Murzyn

8. Client   Ivega Corporation
    Designers   Jean McKenzie & Debbi Murzyn

9. Client   Ernst & Young
    Designers   Jean McKenzie, Debbie Murzyn,
               & Jenny Kolcun

10. Client   Urban Guides
    Designers   Jean McKenzie, Debbie Murzyn,
               & Ada Lee

11. Client   National Theater Workshop
               of the Handicapped
    Designers   Tobin Beck, Christy Beck,
               & Rose Dominiano

12. Client   Kraft Foods
    Designer   Christy Beck

13. Client   WEBS—Foreign Fund, Inc.
    Designer   Kaoru Sato

14. Client   Arroyo Grille
    Designer   Tobin Beck

15. Client   Chase Manhattan Bank
    Designers   Tobin Beck & Christy Beck

1.

▸ **THERE'S MORE IN IT**™ ◂

2.

3.

APC
Professional
We make networks work.

4.

BAY AREA
WATER TRANSIT
INITIATIVE
charting the course

5.

THE **AgBio**

CEO MEETING

6.

1
   Design Firm Elektra Entertainment
2, 3
   Design Firm Miriello Grafico Inc.
4 - 7
   Design Firm McKenzie & Associates, Inc.

1. Client   Vitamin C
     Designer   Alli Truch

2. Client   Hot Z
     Designer   Chris Keeney

3. Client   ezlink
     Designer   Michelle Aranda

4. Client   PC Professional
     Designers Jean McKenzie &
                Debbi Merzyn

5. Client   Bay Area Water Transit
              & Initiative
     Designers Dan Wen & Debbi Merzyn

6. Client   Burrill & Company
     Designers Jean McKenzie & Debbi Merzyn

7. Client   Burrill & Company
     Designers Jean McKenzie & Debbi Merzyn

(opposite)
   Design Firm Hanson Associates, Inc.

   Client   The Eyeglass Works
   Designer   Mary Zook

7.

the eyeglass works

ALTEK

INNOVATIVE
MANUFACTURING
SOLUTIONS

1.

2.

ArborView

RETIREMENT COMMUNITY

Inland Northwest
Cancer Centers

The hope to cure. The promise to care.

3.

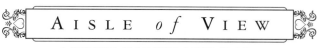

AISLE *of* VIEW

A WEDDING FROM YOUR POINT OF VIEW

4.

E-SYNC networks, inc.

5.

CHRIS L. CHAFFIN, DDS

GENERAL, COSMETIC & IMPLANT DENTISTRY

6.

INTERACTIVE
MINDS

7.

Vubox

8.

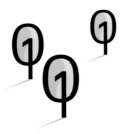

Application
Park™

9.

NETWORKS

10.

shepherd
GOLF

11.

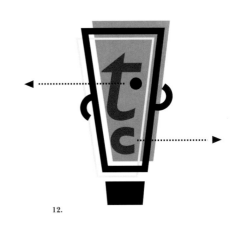

12.

EXTROVERT

13.

14.

microlink

15.

1 - 3, 6
Design Firm Klundt Hosmer Design
4
**Design Firm Graphica
Communication Solutions**
5
Design Firm The Wyant Symbol Group
7, 10, 11
Design Firm Long Design
8, 9
Design Firm Vubox
12 - 15
Design Firm Miriello Grafico Inc.

1. Client   Altek
   Designers Darin Klundt & Tracey Carlson

2. Client   ArborView Retirement
            Community
   Designers Darin Klundt & Brian Gage

3. Client   Inland Northwest
            Cancer Centers
   Designers Darin Klundt &
            Shirlee Bonifield

4. Client   Aisle of View
   Designer Craig Terrones

5. Client   E - Sync Network Systems
   Designers Julia Wyant & Paul Neel

6. Client   Chris L. Chaffin, DDS
   Designers Darin Klundt & Amy Gunter

7. Client   Interactive Minds
   Designer Jennifer Long

8. Client   Vubox
   Designer Robin Awes

9. Client   Application Park
   Designer Robin Awes

10. Client   Redback Networks
    Designer Jennifer Long

11. Client   Shepherd Golf
    Designer Jennifer Long

12. Client   Technically Correct
    Designer Dennis Garcia

13. Client   Extrovert
    Designer Liz Bernal

14. Client   Newport Communications
    Designers Chris Keeney & Dennis Garcia

15. Client   Microlink
    Designer Chris Keeney

Dog Goods, Ltd.

1.

"CHEQUE-6"

2.

inner circle

3.

THE EQUITABLE BUILDING

4.

150
CALIFORNIA
STREET

5.

WHITEHILL

6.

7.

NEW ENGLAND *Builders,* INC.

8.

296

9.

WORLDWIDE
P L A Z A

10.

11.

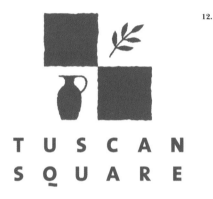

T U S C A N
S Q U A R E

12.

13.

14.

15

1 - 10
Design Firm Pivot Design, Inc.
11, 13 - 15
Design Firm Long Design
12
Design Firm Studio Morris

1. Client   Dog Goods, Ltd.
    Designer   Elizabeth Johnson

2. Client   Cheque 6
                  Aviation Photography
    Designer   Brock Haldeman

3. Client   Focal Communications Corp.
    Designer   Bonnie Caub.e

4. Client   Jones Lang LaSalle
    Designer   Brock Haldeman

5. Client   Equity Office
    Designer   Brock Haldeman

6. Client   Whitehill Technologies
    Designer   Brock Haldeman

7. Client   Uppercase Books
    Designer   Elizabeth Johnson

8. Client   New England Builders, Inc.
    Designer   Tim Hogan

9. Client   Jones Lang LaSalle
    Designer   Brock Haldeman

10. Client   Jones Lang LaSalle
    Designer   Brock Haldeman

11. Client   NetChannel
    Designer   Jennifer Long

12. Client   Tuscan Square
    Designers   Patricia Kovic & Jeff Morris

13. Client   BorrowWise
    Designer   Jennifer Long

14. Client   Electric Minds
    Designer   Jennifer Long

15. Client   arzoon.com
    Designer   Jennifer Long

1.

100%CLUB

2.

Navigator

I N V E S T M E N T S

3.

4.

5.

stil life

NATURAL FURNITURE

6.

MOXIE!
the santa monica film festival

7.

CRI

CONTRACT RECRUITING INC

8.

SHORELINE

TECHNOLOGY PARK

9.

CIVC

PARTNERS

10.

1, 3
Design Firm Adkins/Balhunas
2
Design Firm Hitachi Data Systems
4
Design Firm Rickabaugh Graphics
5 - 8
Design Firm Insyght
9, 10
Design Firm Pivot Design, Inc.

1. Client   Illumination Concepts
    Designers   Jerry Balchunas,
                  Susan DeAngelis &
                  Michelle Phaneuf

2. Client   Hitachi Data Systems
    Designer   Lilia Chu

3. Client   Navigator Investments
    Designers   Jerry Balchunas,
                  Michelle Phaneuf &
                  Matt Fernbuger

4. Client   Vanderbilt University
    Designers   Eric Rickabaugh & Dave Cap

5. Client   Insyght
    Designer   Fabian Geyrhalter

6. Client   Nadeau
    Designer   Fabian Geyrhalter

7. Client   Moxie! The Santa Monica
                  Film Festival
    Designer   Fabian Geyrhalter

8. Client   Contract Recruiting
    Designer   Fabian Geyrhalter

9. Client   Equity Office
    Designer   Brock Haldman

10. Client   CIVC Partners
    Designer   Holle Anderson

INLAND NORTHWEST HEALTH SERVICES

3.

1.

4.

5.

6.

2.

7.

8.

PROGRESSIVE
LENDING LLC

9.

10.

11.

12.

13.

Cancer
Patient
Care

14.

15.

1, 2
Design Firm Rickabaugh Graphics
3 - 15
Design Firm Klundt Hosmer Design

1. Client   Seton Hall University
    Designer   Eric Rickabaugh

2. Client   Seton Hall University
    Designers   Eric Rickabaugh & Dave Cap

3. Client   Inland Northwest
                  Health Services
    Designers   Darin Klundt & Henry Ortega

4. Client   Intermountain Forest Assoc.
    Designers   Darin Klundt & Amy Gunter

5. Client   Whitworth
    Designers   Brian Gage & Darin Klundt

6. Client   Providence Services of E.W.
    Designers   Darin Klundt & Henry Ortega

7. Client   Spokane Skills Center
    Designers   Darin Klundt & Amy Gunter

8. Client   North by Northwest
                  Entertainment
    Designers   Darin Klundt & Brian Gage

9. Client   Progressive Lending
    Designers   Darin Klundt &
                  Judy Heggum-Davis

10. Client   The Basket
    Designer   Brian Gage

11. Client   Mel
    Designers   Brian Gage & Darin Klundt

12. Client   North Pointe
                  Retirement Community
    Designers   Darin Klundt & Brian Gage

13. Client   MacKay Manufacturing
    Designers   Darin Klundt & Brian Gage

14. Client   Cancer Patient Care
    Designers   Darin Klundt & Amy Gunter

15. Client   Aurora Consulting Group
    Designers   Darin Klundt , Judy
                  Heggum-Davis, & Brian Gage

1.

2.

3.

4.

5.

6.

1 - 3
  **Design Firm Babcock, Schmid, Louis,
           & Partners**
4
  Design Firm Iron Design
5
  Design Firm Long Design
6, 7
  Design Firm Klundt Hosmer Design

1. Client   Minit Mart
    Designers   Babcock, Schmid, Louis,
                  & Partners

2. Client   Minit Mart
    Designers   Babcock, Schmid, Louis,
                  & Partners

3. Client   Minit Mart
    Designers   Babcock, Schmid, Louis,
                  & Partners

4. Client   Metropolitan Foundation
    Designer   Todd Edmonds

5. Client   Rhonda Abrams
    Designer   Jennifer Long

6. Client   Desautel Hege Communications
    Designers   Darin Klundt & Henry Ortega

7. Client   Executive Lending Group
    Designers   Brian Gage & Darin Klundt

(opposite)
  Design Firm Wallace Church Ass., Inc.

    Client   Maxfli Golf Balls
    Designers   Stan Church, John Waski,
                  & Derek Samue

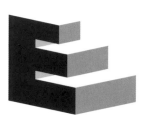

7.

USA Asian Pacific Trading, LLC

1.

2.

3.

4.

5.

Advantagekbs

6.

7.

8.

9.

10.

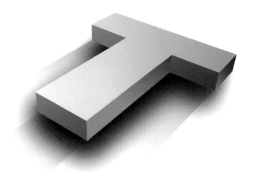

11.

12.

BUMBLE BEE

13.

ADP® YEAR 2000 COMPLIANCE
2000 PROGRAM 1999

14.

OpenCon Systems, Inc.
WORLDWIDE COMMUNICATIONS SOLUTIONS

15.

1 - 4
Design Firm **Babcock, Schmid, Louis & Partners**
5
Design Firm **Imageignition**
6 - 8, 14, 15
Design Firm **David Morris Creative Inc.**
9 - 13
Design Firm **Wallace Church Ass., Inc.**

1. Client — U.S.A. Asian Pacific Trading
   Designers — Babcock, Schmid, Louis & Partners

2. Client — Bob Evans
   Designers — Babcock, Schmid, Louis & Partners

3. Client — Audio Technica
   Designers — Babcock, Schmid, Louis & Partners

4. Client — Krystal
   Designers — Babcock, Schmid, Louis & Partners

5. Client — La Casa Films
   Designer — Adrian Bellesguard

6. Client — Advantage Kbs
   Designer — Glenn Gontha

7. Client — OCS - Open Con Systems
   Designer — Denise Spirito

8. Client — Corporate Computing Expo
   Designer — Glenn Gontha

9. Client — The Axis Group, IIC
   Designers — Stan Church, Wendy Church, & Lucian Toma

10. Client — Lycos
    Designers — Stan Church & Craig Swanson

11. Client — Tri-State Graphics
    Designers — Stan Church, Wendy Church, & Lucian Toma

12. Client — Green Media Cultivation
    Designers — Nin Glaister & Paula Bunny

13. Client — Bumble Bee Tuna
    Designers — Stan Church & Diana King

14. Client — ADP
    Designer — Matt Gilbert

15. Client — OCS - Open Con Systems
    Designer — Matt Gilbert

CITADEL
MALL

1.

MISSION
2

2.

N O R T H W O O D S
MALL

3.

R
Regency Mall

4.

Southlake Mall

5.

6.

7.

8.

9.

10.

11.

12.

13.

14.

15.

(all)

Design Firm Herip Associates

1. Client   The Richard E. Jacobs Group
   Designers Walter M. Herip, John R.
             Menter, & Rick Holb

2. Client   The Richard E. Jacobs Group
   Designers John R. Menter &
             Walter M. Herip

3. Client   The Richard E. Jacobs Group
   Designers John R. Menter, Rick Holb,
             & Walter M. Herip

4, 5
   Client   The Richard E. Jacobs Group
   Designers John R. Menter &
             Walter M. Herip

6 - 8
   Client   Cleveland Indians
   Designers John R. Menter &
             Walter M. Herip

9, 10
   Client   Major League Baseball
   Designers Walter M. Herip &
             John R. Menter

11. Client   CVNRA
    Designers Walter M. Herip

12. Client   Ernst & Young, LLP
    Designers Walter M. Herip &
              John R. Menter

13. Client   Dalad Group
    Designers John R. Menter &
              Walter M. Herip

14. Client   Bioproducts, Inc.
    Designers Walter M. Herip, John R.
              Menter, & Rick Holb

15. Client   Stark Enterprises
    Designers Walter M. Herip, John R.
              Menter, & Rick Holb

1.

2.

3.

4.

Smyth **S**pecialty **S**ervices

5.

6.

7.

8.

9.

10.

11.

13.

12.

14.

15.

1 - 3
Design Firm   **Ray Braun Graphic Design**
4
Design Firm   **Farenga Design Group**
5
Design Firm   **Graphx Design**
6 - 13
Design Firm   **Todd Nickel**
14, 15
Design Firm   **Herip Associates**

1. Client   Exodus International
   Designer   Ray Braun

2. Client   Everett Gospel Mission
   Designer   Ray Braun

3. Client   Seattle Pacific University
   Designer   Ray Braun

4. Client   Watson-Guptill Publications
   Designer   Anthony Farenga

5. Client   Smyth Specialty Services, LLC
   Designers   Patrick Smith & Alex Sobie

6. Client   North Atlantic Services
   Designer   Todd Nickel

7. Client   Skipper's Restaurant
   Designer   Todd Nickel

8. Client   GOLFDOME
   Designer   Todd Nickel

9 - 11
   Client   Sugar Beats
   Designer   Todd Nickel

12. Client   MS. PC
    Designer   Todd Nickel

13. Client   Green Dreams
    Designer   Todd Nickel

14. Client   Herip Associates
    Designer   Walter M. Herip

15. Client   The Richard E. Jacobs Group
    Designers   Walter M. Herip &
                John R. Meter

THE HEARING
Advocate

1.

THE HEARING
ADVOCATE

2.

WOOD
TRADER

3.

4.

5.

out 🌙
HOUSE
STUDIO
graphics, art & design

6.

SUCCESS
at FELICIAN
ACCELERATED DEGREE PROGRAMS

7.

1, 2, 4 - 7
Design Firm Outhouse Studio
3
Design Firm Nesnadny + Schwartz

1, 2
  Client   Ingroup Networking
  Designers Alex Lindquist & Jolanta Hyjek

3. Client   WoodTrader
   Designers Timothy Lachina, Gregory
             Oznowich, & Brian Lavy

4. Client   Entertainment Management
   Designers Alex Lindquist & Jolanta Hyjek

5. Client   Pulse Plastic Products, Inc.
   Designers Alex Lindquist & Jolanta Hyjek

6. Client   Outhouse Studio
   Designer   Alex Lindquist

7. Client   Ingroup Networking
   Designer   Alex Lindquist

(opposite)
Design Firm Larsen Design + Interactive

   Client   Larsen's I'm Y2OK Campaign
   Designers Tim Larsen, Sascha Boecker,
             & Elise Williams

1.

2.

3.

4.

5.

6.

7.

8.

9.

10.

11.

12.

13.

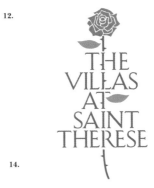

14.

VALUE CITY ARENA

JEROME
SCHOTTENSTEIN
CENTER

15.

1
Design Firm Larsen Design + Interactive
2 - 15
Design Firm Rickabaugh Graphics

1. Client   Minnesota Parks &
                 Trails Council
    Designer   Todd Mannes

2. Client   Atticus Scribe
    Designer   Eric Rickabaugh

3. Client   The Ball Busters
    Designer   Eric Rickabaugh

4. Client   Buckeye Hall of Fame Cafe
    Designer   Eric Rickabaugh

5. Client   Celine Dion
    Designer   Eric Rickabaugh

6. Client   The Columbus Quest
    Designer   Eric Rickabaugh

7. Client   Drexel University
    Designers   Eric Rickabaugh & Rod Smith

8. Client   University Laundry &
                 Dry Cleaning
    Designers   Eric Rickabaugh & Dave Cap

9. Client   Your Money Magazine
    Designer   Eric Rickabaugh

10. Client   Your Money Magazine
    Designers   Eric Rickabaugh & Dave Cap

11. Client   Ohio State Motorsports
    Designers   Eric Rickabaugh &
                 Anthony Mosca

12. Client   Nationwide Insurance
    Designer   Eric Rickabaugh

13. Client   The Southern Theatre
    Designer   Eric Rickabaugh

14. Client   The Catholic Diocese
    Designer   Eric Rickabaugh

15. Client   The Ohio State University
    Designer   Eric Rickabaugh

1.

2.

nexen™

3.

THE MINNEAPOLIS INSTITUTE OF ARTS

4.

6.

Gartner**Institute**

5.

GREAT PLAINS

1 - 7

Design Firm   Larsen Design + Interactive

1. Client   Minnesota Interactive
                Marketing Association
   Designers   Richelle J. Huff, Emily Eaton,
                & Peter Langlais

2. Client   Agiliti
   Designers   Paul Wharton & Brad Serum

3. Client   Nexen
   Designers   Jo Davison & Bill Pflipsen

4. Client   The Minneapolis
                Institute of Arts
   Designers   Todd Nesser, Peter de Sibour,
                Todd Mannes, Pepa Reimann,
                & Mark Wagner

5. Client   Gartner Institute
   Designers   Paul Wharton & Todd Mannes

6. Client   Great Plains Software
   Designers   Richelle J. Huff, Mike Haug,
                Bill Pflipsen, Sascha Boeker,
                Chad Amon, & Michael Hersrud

7. Client   21 North Main
   Designers   Jo Davison, Mark Saunders,
                & Todd Nesser

(opposite)
Design Firm   Larsen Design + Interactive

   Client   Target
   Designers   Paul Wharton, Peter de Sibour,
                & Chris Zastoupil

7.

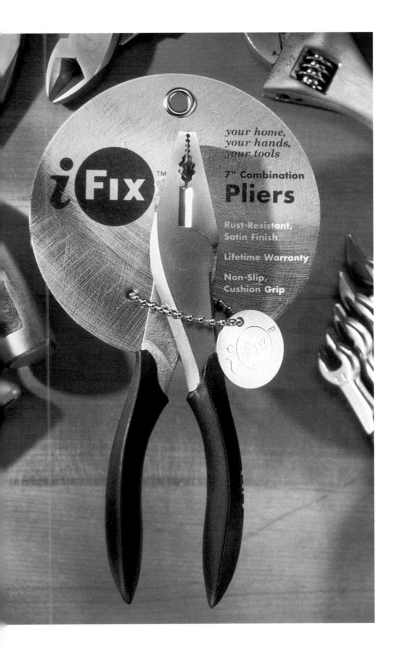

*your home,
your hands,
your tools*

iFix™

**7" Combination
Pliers**

Rust-Resistant,
Satin Finish

Lifetime Warranty

Non-Slip,
Cushion Grip

iFix™

*your home,
your hands,
your tools*

iFix™

**8" Adjustable
Wrench**

SAE and Metric
Lifetime Warranty
Non-Slip, Cushi

1.

California Association of
Professional Employees

2.

GRAMMY
AWARDS
February 23, 2000
8 pm, ET/PT on CBS

3.

TAIX

French
Country
Cuisine
Established 1927

4.

ROYAL HEALTH CARE

5.

EASTERN WOMEN'S CENTER
security, sensitivity, support...

6.

redapt

7.

the summit
2000 oho

8.

316

9.   10.

11.   12.

13.

14.

15.

1 - 6
Design Firm **Mark Deitch & Associates, Inc.**
7, 8, 10 - 13
Design Firm **Tim Celeski Studios**
9
Design Firm **Nesnadny + Schwartz**
14 - 15
Design Firm **Adkins/Balchunas**

1. Client   CAPE
   Designer   Sara Patterson

2. Client   NARAS
   Designer   Raoul Pascual

3. Client   National Hydrogen Association
   Designer   Lisa Kokenis

4. Client   Taix Restaurant
   Designers Radul Pascual & Joe Ibarra

5. Client   Royal Health Care
   Designer   Lisa Kokenis

6. Client   Eastern Women's Center
   Designer   Lisa Kokenis

7. Client   Redapt Systems & Peripherals
   Designer   Tim Celeski

8. Client   Small Office/Home Office
   Designer   Tim Celeski

9. Client   Urban Feast
   Designers Joyce Nesnadny, Cindy Lowrey,
              & Michelle Moehler

10. Client   Terabeam Corporation
    Designer Tim Celeski

11. Client   Producebiz. com
    Designer Tim Celeski

12. Client   Innovation
    Designer Tim Celeski

13. Client   2Way Corporation
    Designer Tim Celeski

14. Client   Sbarro
    Designers Jerry Balchunas &
              Susan DeAngelis

15. Client   Sbarro
    Designers Jerry Balchunas & Steve Rebello

317

1.

CLICKMOVIE.COM

2.

master printing

3.

4.

5.

6.

7.

8.

318

WYSE•LANDAU

9.

10.

THE CORAL COMPANY

11.

12.

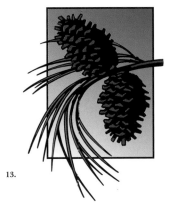

13.

SMITH+Co

14.

15.

1, 2
Design Firm Derek Yee Design
3, 8 - 11, 15
Design Firm Nesnadny + Schwartz
4 - 7
Design Firm D4 Creative Group
12 - 14
Design Firm Michael Courtney Design

1. Client   Click Movie.com
   Designer   Derek Yee

2. Client   Oracle
   Designer   Derek Yee

3. Client   Master Printing, Inc.
   Designers   Cindy Lowrey & Stacie Ross

4. Client   Radio Wall Street
   Designer   Wicky W. Lee

5. Client   E Flooring Plus
   Designer   Wicky W. Lee

6. Client   Fins Philadelphia
   Designer   Wicky W. Lee

7. Client   D4 Creative Group
   Designer   Wicky W. Lee

8. Client   Hengst Streff Bajko Architects
   Designers   Timothy Lachina, Michelle
                Mohler & Gregory Oznowich

9. Client   Wyse Landau Public Relations
   Designers   Joyce Nesnadny &
                Michelle Mohler

10. Client   Coral Company
    Designers   Cindy Lowerey & Stacie Ross

11. Client   Crossey International
    Designer   Joyce Nesnadny

12. Client   Fleischmann Office Interiors
    Designers   Michael Courtney, Dan Hoang,
                Heidi Favour, & Brian O'Neill

13. Client   Evergreen Printing
    Designer   Michael Courtney

14. Client   Smith & Co.
    Designers   Michael Courtney &
                Brian O'Neill

15. Client   Cleveland Zoological Society
    Designers   Timothy Lachina &
                Gregory Oznowich

1.

ACES
Academic Competence
Evaluation Scales™

2.

Symmorphix

3.

Derek Yee **Design**

4.

a!
apress

5.

6.

7.

(opposite)
Design Firm Adkins/Balchunas

Client   The Groceria
Designers   Jerry Balchunas &
              Michelle Phaneuf

1, 2
Design Firm Clockwork Design
3 - 7
Design Firm Derek Yee Design

1. Client   Outdoors Almanac
   Designers   Steve Gaines & Terri Gaines

2. Client   The Psychological Corporation
   Designers   Steve Gaines & Terri Gaines

3. Client   Symmorphix
   Designers   Derek Yee, Elysia Chuh,
              & Philip So

4. Client   Derek Yee Design
   Designer   Derek Yee

5. Client   Apress
   Designers   Derek Yee, Elysia Chuh,
              & Seiko Nozaki

6. Client   America Online
   Designer   Derek Yee

7. Client   Oracle
   Designers   Elysia Chuh & Derek Yee

CLOCKWORK DESIGN

1.

2.

GlobalNet

3.

N/M

4.

RAYDAR.COM

5.

THE CHAMBER
Chamber Challenge
4TH ANNUAL GOLF TOURNAMENT
CANYON SPRINGS

6.

SAFC

7.

Velotools

8.

Beta III

9.

10.

SENSORY PROFILE

11.

DRAGONS
ASPHALT ASSAULT
summer tour 98

12.

Thera Games ™

13.

T S D

14.

S
SPECTRUM
LANDSCAPING

15.

1 - 9, 11 - 15
Design Firm Clockwork Design
10
Design Firm Look

1.	Client	Clockwork Design
	Designers	Steve Gaines & Terri Gaines
2.	Client	Foresight Consulting Inc.
	Designers	Steve Gaines & Terri Gaines
3.	Client	GlobalNet
	Designers	Steve Gaines & Terri Gaines
4.	Client	New Millennium Consulting
	Designers	Steve Gaines & Terri Gaines
5.	Client	Raydar.com
	Designers	Steve Gaines & Terri Gaines
6.	Client	San Antonio Chamber of Commerce
	Designers	Steve Gaines & Terri Gaines
7.	Client	San Antonio Football Club
	Designer	Steve Gaines

8.	Client	Velotools
	Designers	Steve Gaines & Terri Gaines
9.	Client	The Psychological Corporation
	Designers	Steve Gaines & Terri Gaines
10.	Client	Look
	Designer	Betsy Todd
11.	Client	The Psychological Corporation
	Designers	Steve Gaines & Terri Gaines
12.	Client	San Antonio Dragons
	Designers	Steve Gaines & Terri Gaines
13.	Client	The Psychological Corporation
	Designers	Steve Gaines & Terri Gaines
14.	Client	Total Systems Development
	Designers	Steve Gaines & Terri Gaines
15.	Client	Spectrum Landscaping
	Designers	Steve Gaines & Terri Gaines

1.

2.

Solid Wood. Solid Quality. Ready-to-Finish Furniture!

3.

TERRE HAUTE
INTERNATIONAL AIRPORT
HULMAN FIELD

4.

5.

FirstMile
TECHNOLOGIES

6.

7.

1
Design Firm Dennis S. Juett &
              Associates Inc.
2 - 6
Design Firm Miller & White Adv., Inc.
7
Design Firm Clockwork Design

1. Client   Allen Lund Company
   Designer   Dennis S. Juett

2. Client   Country Living
   Designers Bill White & Tim Keller

3. Client   Terre Haute
              International Airport
   Designers Brian Miller & Bruce Morgan

4. Client   Doughmakers
   Designers Brian Miller, Bruce Morgan,
              & Tim Keller

5. Client   Estridge
   Designer   Brian Miller & Bruce Morgan

6. Client   Leagre Chandler & Millard
   Designers Bill White & Bruce Morgan

7. Client   Bexar Metropolotan
              Water District
   Designers Steve Gaines & Terri Gaines

(opposite)
Design Firm Hitachi Data Systems

   Client   Hitachi Data Systems
   Designer   Kim Ocumen

Together,
we **can** create
miracles

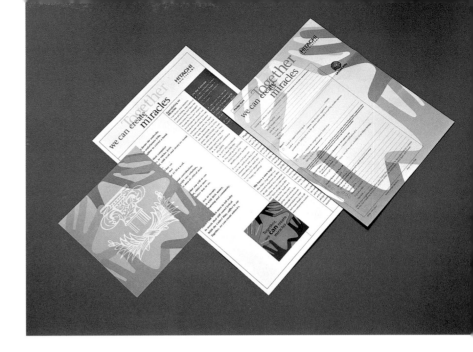

HDS 1998-99 United Way Campa

Together,
we **can** create
miracles

SNΛPP
& ASSOCIATES
ARCHITECTURAL DESIGN TEAM

1.

neolinx.com

2.

3.

A PARTNER IN THE
UNION HOSPITAL HEALTH GROUP

4.

5.

6.

7.

8.

9.

10.

VOLUNTEER
Pasadena Police Foundation Sponsor

11.

12.

MOSIS

13.

FALL FOOD & WINE

14.

THE
ATHENAEUM
FUND

15.

1.

2.

3.

4.

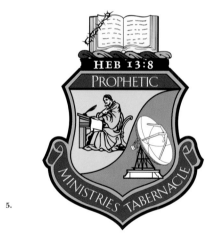

5.

6.

7.

8.

328

9.

10.

HITACHI DATA SYSTEMS KICKOFF '99

11.

12.

iLAB

13.

XAVIER
MUSKETEERS

14.

15.

L.

2.

3.

YU'S CHIP CORP

4.

PRINCE
INVESTMENTS

5.

6.

7.

1
Design Firm **Adkins/Balchunas**
2 - 5
Design Firm **Vivatt Design Group**
6, 7
Design Firm **Mark Deitch &**
Associates, Inc.

1. Client   Sbarro
   Designers   Jerry Balchunas &
               Michelle Phaneuf

2. Client   HI-VAL
   Designer   Dan Wen

3. Client   Yu's Chip Corp.
   Designer   Dan Wen

4. Client   Inwin Development, Inc.
   Designer   Dan Wen

5. Client   Prince Investments
   Designer   Dan Wen

6. Client   UCLA Medical School
   Designers   Lisa Kokenis & Joe Ibarra

7. Client   Landsman, Frank & Bloch
   Designer   Raoul Pascual

(opposite)
Design Firm **Adkins/Balchunas**

Client   Autocrat, Inc.
Designers   Jerry Balchunas, Michelle
            Phaneuf, & Susan DeAngelis

1.

2.

3.

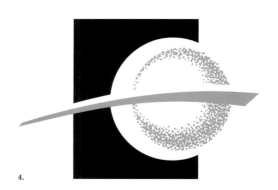

4.

5.

6.

7.

8.

9.

10.

11.

12.

13.

14.

actos™

15.

1 - 7
Design Firm   Dever Designs
8 - 15
Design Firm   CMC Design Associates

1. Client   Diamanti
    Designer   Jeffrey L. Dever

2. Client   Institute of Museum &
                Library Services
    Designer   Jeffrey L. Dever

3. Client   Martin's Furniture
    Designers   Emily Martin Kendall &
                Jeffrey L. Dever

4. Client   Carnegie Endowment for
                International Peace
    Designers   Jeffrey L. Dever &
                Emily Martin Kendall

5. Client   American Association
                of Museums
    Designer   Jeffrey L. Dever

6. Client   American Association of
                Physician Assistants
    Designer   Jeffrey L. Dever

7. Client   American Gas Association
    Designer   Jeffrey L. Dever

8. Client   Abelson-Taylor, Inc.
    Designer   Chris Cacci

9. Client   Spectrum Research &
                Development
    Designer   Chris Cacci

10. Client   Center for Fertility &
                Reproduction
    Designer   Chris Cacci

11. Client   Heart Source
    Designer   Chris Cacci

12. Client   Trimark Technologies
    Designer   Chris Cacci

13. Client   B & M Management
    Designer   Chris Cacci

14. Client   Center for Speech &
                Language Disorders
    Designer   Chris Cacci

15. Client   Abelson-Taylor, Inc./Lilly
    Designer   Chris Cacci

VIVATT
design group

1.

2.

3.

ASTRA DATA

4.

TONE YEE
INVESTMENTS & DEVELOPMENTS

5.

6.

1 - 7
Design Firm Vivatt Design Group
8, 9
Design Firm Hornall Anderson
Design Works

1. Client   Vivatt Design Group
   Designers   Dan Wen & Steven Wei

2. Client   Realworld Technology, Inc.
   Designer   Eric Woo

3. Client   Computer 411
   Designer   Eric Woo

4. Client   Astra Data
   Designer   Dan Wen

5. Client   Tone Yee
               Investment & Developments
   Designer   Dan Wen

6. Client   QRUN
   Designer   Dan Wen

7. Client   Yus Group
   Designer   Dan Wen

8. Client   Food Services of America
   Designers   Jack Anderson, Cliff Chung,
               Heidi Favour, Debra McCloskey,
               & Julie Lock

9. Client   Tigerlily
   Designers   Jack Anderson, Lisa Cerveny,
               Sonja Max, & Mary Hermes

7.

8.

9.

Hallin
CONSTRUCTION
CONSULTING

1.

SHOOT
THE
ROCK
Roundball
Tournament

2.

Rockford
Symphony
Orchestra
Guild

3.

ORION

4.

CWS

5.

ACCLAIM TECHNOLOGY

6.

iMIX

7.

TOYO
SYSTEMS USA INC.

8.

WIRELESSHQ

9.

C●MMPAGE

10.

SUNP●WER

11.

STENDMAR

12.

Elliott

13.

Dēglass furniture

14.

EQUALTRADE
INTERNATIONAL CORP

15.

1 - 3		
Design Firm	**Conflux Design**	
4		
Design Firm	**Adam Design**	
5, 6		
Design Firm	**Fine Design Group**	
7 - 15		
Design Firm	**Vivatt Design Group**	
1.	Client	Hallin Construction Consulting
	Designer	Grey Fedore
2.	Client	Rock Valley College Foundation
	Designer	Grey Fedore
3.	Client	Rockford Symphony Orchestra Guild
	Designers	Grey Fedore & Scott Fustin
4.	Client	Orion
	Designer	Adam Rozum
5.	Client	Cool World Sports
	Designer	Ed Andrews
6.	Client	Acclaim Technology
	Designer	John Taylor

7.	Client	Netlink Technology
	Designer	Steven Wei
8.	Client	Toyo Systems
	Designer	Steven Wei
9.	Client	Wireless HQ
	Designer	Steven Wei
10.	Client	Commpage
	Designer	Steven Wei
11.	Client	Sunpower
	Designer	Steven Wei
12.	Client	Vivatt Design Group
	Designer	Steven Wei
13.	Client	NETcellent Systems
	Designer	Steven Wei
14.	Client	Déglass Furniture
	Designer	Eric Woo
15.	Client	Equaltrade International Corp.
	Designer	Eric Woo

1.

2.

TheBRIDGE
CONNECTING PEOPLE, PROCESS AND PERFORMANCE

3.

CUSTOMER
OPERATIONS

4.

Your Personal Access Line
HR DIRECT

5.

IRIS

6.

7.

Quantum Leaps,
No Bounds.

Littlefield
UNLIMITED
SPECIALTY · MARKETING

8.

9.

10.

11.

12.

GLOBAL GOURMET CATERING

13.

c a p s t a n

14.

BREAD WORKSHOP

15.

1, 3 - 5, 11		
Design Firm	**Ervin Marketing**	
	Creative Communications	
2, 6 - 10		
Design Firm	**Whitney Stinger, Inc.**	
12 - 15		
Design Firm	**Fine Design Group**	

1.	Client	Clayton Chamber of Commerce
	Designers	Mike Whitney & Lisa Markham
2.	Client	Trainwreck
	Designer	Mike Whitney
3.	Client	Hoechst
	Designers	Mike Whitney & Jean Gorea
4.	Client	Ford Motor Co.
	Designers	Mike Whitney & Jean Corea
5.	Client	Warner-Lambert
	Designers	Mike Whitney & Jean Corea
6.	Client	Iris Whitney
	Designer	Mike Whitney

7.	Client	Julie Gustafson Words That Work
	Designers	Mike Whitney & Karl Stinger
8.	Client	Littlefield Unlimited
	Designer	Mike Whitney & Karl Stinger
9.	Client	Littlefield Unlimited
	Designer	Mike Whitney
10.	Client	Littlefield Unlimited
	Designer	Mike Whitney
11.	Client	Malarky's
	Designer	Mike Whitney
12.	Client	Fine Design Group
	Designer	Marcela Barrientos
13.	Client	Global Gourmet Catering
	Designer	Megan Stohr
14.	Client	Capstan
	Designer	John Taylor
15.	Client	Bread Workshop
	Designers	Jake Barlow, John Taylor, & Kenn Fine

Hellmann **Photography**

1.

BookQuest®

2.

school of information studies

3.

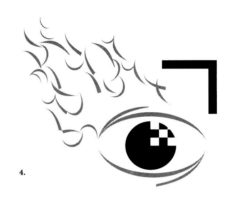

4.

ALTERNATIVE
HEALING
CENTER

5.

6.

7.

(opposite)
Design Firm   **Hornall Anderson Design Works**

Client   Wells Fargo "innoVisions"
Designers   Jack Anderson, Kathy Saito, Alan Copeland, & Cliff Chung

1 - 7
Design Firm   **Adam Design**

1.   Client   Hellmann Photography
   Designer   Adam Rozum

2.   Client   BookQuest
   Designer   Adam Rozum

3.   Client   School of Information Studies
   Designer   Adam Rozum

4.   Client   Photofusion
   Designer   Adam Rozum

5.   Client   Alternative Healing Center
   Designer   Adam Rozum

6.   Client   Saranac Software
   Designer   Adam Rozum

7.   Client   People on Design
   Designer   Adam Rozum

pixelprecision

1.

APT

2.

Force5™
software

3.

PanelLink®
D I G I T A L

4.

jcloak™

5.

SIA
SEMICONDUCTOR
INDUSTRY
ASSOCIATION

6.

Chamber of Commerce
MOUNTAIN VIEW

7.

MDVista™

8.

DESIGN SOLUTIONS
FOR THE WORKPLACE

9.

SINCE 1960 **PFG**™
POLLOCK FINANCIAL GROUP

10.

11.

12.

13.

14.

en Vision identity, inc.

15.

(all)
Design Firm   en Vision Identity, Inc.

1. Client   Pixel Precision
   Designer   Karl Kromer

2. Client   APT
   Designer   Vadim Goretsky

3. Client   Force 5 software
   Designer   Shepherd Brown

4. Client   PanelLink Digital
   Designer   Erin Mathis

5. Client   Force 5 software
   Designer   Shepherd Brown

6. Client   Semiconductor Industry
                 Association
   Designer   Karl Kromer

7. Client   Mountain View
                 Chamber of Commerce
   Designers   Nicole Bloss & Iva Dasovic

8. Client   MD Vista
   Designer   Nicole Bloss

9. Client   aai
   Designer   Karl Kromer &
                 Shepherd Brown

10. Client   Pollock Financial Group
    Designer   Vadim Goretsky

11. Client   See U There
    Designer   Karl Kromer

12. Client   i am networks
    Designer   Karl Kromer

13. Client   eBalance, inc.
    Designer   Nicole Bloss

14. Client   PowerClient
    Designer   Nicole Bloss

15. Client   en Vision identity, inc.
    Designer   Nicole Bloss

1.

2.

DIVERSITY FORUM

MOUNTAIN VIEW

3.

4.

Wedgewood Vision

RANGES & COOKTOPS

5.

Atwood
Compliance
Systems

6.

1, 2
Design Firm   Ocean Avenue Design
3, 4
Design Firm   en Vision identity, inc.
5 - 7
Design Firm   Conflux Design

1. Client   Howlett Surfboards
   Designer   Lynn E. Phillips

2. Client   Blue Sphere
   Designer   Lynn E. Phillips

3. Client   Diversity Forum
                Mountain View
   Designer   Shepherd Brown

4. Client   Silicon Image
   Designers   Nicole Bloss &
                Shepherd Brown

5. Client   Atwood Mobile Products
   Designer   Greg Fedorev

6. Client   Atwood Mobile Products
   Designer   Greg Fedorev

7. Client   Starlight Theatre
   Designer   Greg Fedorev

(opposite)
Design Firm   Squires & Company

Client   Fast Park
Designer   Veronica Vaughn

7.

345

1.

2.

3.

4.

5.

6.

7.

8.

9.

10. CycleSolutions

In Fiore

11.

12.

13.

HOWLETT
surfboards

14.

SHADOWCREST
PUBLICATIONS

15.

ILI◁D

1.

2.

3.

M.A. Weatherbie & Co., Inc.

4.

5.

6.

7.

SCHREFFLER &
ASSOCIATES 🏛

8.

9.

10.

11.

CARE
MANAGEMENT
GROUP
OF GREATER
NEW YORK, INC.℠

12.

13.

BRANY

GRACEHOPPER

14.

15.

1
Design Firm   **Sibley Peteet Design**
2 - 15
Design Firm   **inc3**

1. Client   Chase Bank
   Designer   Tom Hough

2. Client   inc3
   Designers   Harvey Appelbaum &
   Nick Guarracino

3. Client   ESCC
   Designers   Harvey Appelbaum &
   Nick Guarracino

4. Client   M. A. Weatherbie & Co.
   Designers   Harvey Appelbaum &
   Nick Guarracino

5. Client   Unetra Systems
   Designers   Harvey Appelbaum &
   Nick Guarracino

6. Client   North Shore
   Designers   Harvey Appelbaum &
   Nick Guarracino

7. Client   The Atheletic Club
   Designers   Harvey Appelbaum &
   Valerie Viola

8. Client   Schreffler & Associates
   Designers   Harvey Appelbaum &
   Nick Guarracino

9. Client   J - K Orthotics & Prosthetics
   Designers   Harvey Appelbaum &
   Nick Guarracino

10. Client   Pzena Investment Management
    Designers   Harvey Appelbaum &
    Nick Guarracino

11. Client   Care Management Group
    Designers   Harvey Appelbaum &
    Nick Guarracino

12. Client   ERE
    Designers   Harvey Appelbaum &
    Nick Guarracino

13. Client   Biomedical Research Assoc.
    of NY
    Designers   Harvey Appelbaum &
    Nick Guarracino

14. Client   Gracehopper
    Designers   Harvey Appelbaum &
    Nick Guarracino

15. Client   Supermarkets To Go
    Designers   Harvey Appelbaum &
    Nick Guarracino

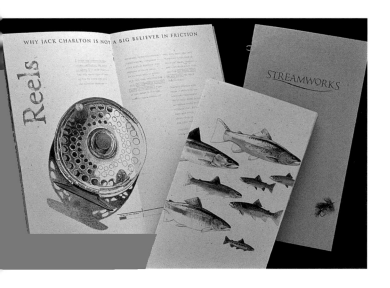

1.

conversā

2.

SINCE 1951

U.S. CIGAR

SALES, INC.

3.

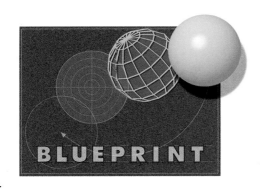

4.

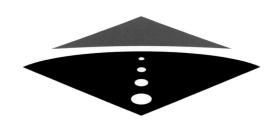

5.

6.

7.

8.

KAMINSKI

9.

10.

1 - 3
Design Firm   **Hornall Anderson Design Works**

4 - 10
Design Firm   **Sibley Peteet Design**

1. Client   Streamworks
   Designers   Jack Anderson, Belinda Bowline, Andrew Smith, & Ed Lee

2. Client   Conversa
   Designers   Jack Anderson, Kathy Saito, & Alan Copeland

3. Client   U.S. Cigar
   Designers   Jack Anderson, Larry Anderson, Mary Hermes, Mike Calkins, & Michael Brugman

4. Client   THE SABRE GROUP
   Designer   Brent McMahan

5. Client   Trans Solutions
   Designer   Joy Price

6. Client   Skin Ceuticals
   Designer   Joy Price

7. Client   Bentonville Public Library
   Designer   David Beck

8. Client   Baker Bros
   Designer   Tom Hough

9. Client   Karen Kaminski
   Designer   Roger Ferris

10. Client   John Hutton
    Designer   Brent McMahan

THE
AUGUSTA
INSTITUTES

The Cornerstone of Motorola's Future

1.

Match-Link®

2.

MOONLIGHT AT MEDINAH

A gala evening to benefit the American Cancer Society

3.

MAGNOLIA STREET
KITCHEN

4.

b

BaerDesignGroup

5.

6.

Premier

7.

8.

9.

10.

THE OAKMARK FAMILY *of* FUNDS

11.

HARLOW & ASSOCIATES P.C.
Certified Public Accountants • Tax Consultants

12.

13.

14.

15.

1 - 5, 9 - 15
Design Firm Baer Design Group
6 - 8
Design Firm Wild Onion Design, Inc.

1. Client	Motorola University	
Designers	Todd D. Baer, Dominy Burkhart, & Julie Rigby	
2. Client	Cendant	
Designer	Todd D. Baer	
3. Client	American Cancer Society	
Designer	Todd D. Baer	
4. Client	Haagen Grocers	
Designer	Todd D. Baer	
5. Client	Baer Design Group	
Designers	Geoff Stone, Dominy Burkhart, & Todd D. Baer	
6. Client	Wild Onion Design Inc.	
Designer	Barbara Inzinga	
7. Client	Premier Auto Finance, Inc.	
Designer	Barbara Inzinga	

8. Client	Professional Organization for Association Executives
Designer	Barbara Inzinga
9. Client	Kayak Jack
Designer	Todd D. Baer
10. Client	Hinsdale Pain Specialists
Designer	Toy Nakajima
11. Client	Harris Associates LLP
Designer	Todd D. Baer
12. Client	Harlow & Associates
Designer	Todd D. Baer
13. Client	Harper College
Designer	Dominy Burkhart
14. Client	Haagen Grocers
Designer	Todd D. Baer
15. Client	Food Club
Designer	Todd D. Baer

THE INNOVATIVE ALE

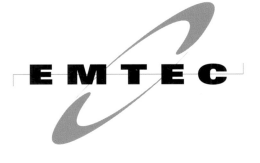

354

1.

CompuChair

2.

MOUNTAIN
trading co.

3.

baskets
BY DESIGN

4.

5.

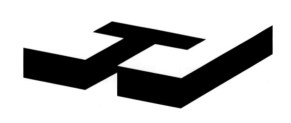

6.

7.

1 - 3		
Design Firm	**Nova Creative Group, Inc.**	
4 - 10		
Design Firm	**Graphica**	
	Communication Solutions	

1. Client	Dover Partners, Inc.
Designer	Kris Hosbein
2. Client	Nova Creative Group, Inc.
Designer	Tim O'Hare
3. Client	EMTEC
Designer	Jack Denlinger
4. Client	Best In Bows
Designer	Craig Terrones

5. Client	CompuChair
Designers	Craig Terrones &
	Robin Walker
6. Client	Mountain Trading Co.
Designer	Craig Terrones
7. Client	Baskets by Design
Designers	Robin Walker &
	Craig Terrones
8. Client	Jaenicke, Inc.
Designer	Craig Terrones
9. Client	Tarragon
Designer	Craig Terrones
10. Client	Solid Vision, Inc.
Designer	Christa Fleming

SunflowerMusic

1.

2.

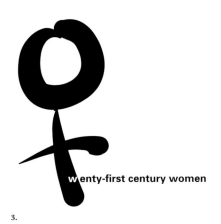

twenty-first century women

3.

4.

5.

print promotions, inc

6.

LEAD DOG
DESIGN & DEVELOPMENT

7.

8.

9.

10.

11.

12.

13.

14.

440A FINE™
Chicago Cutlery

15.

1 - 7
Design Firm Lead Dog Design
8
Design Firm The Font Office Inc.
9 - 13
**Design Firm Graphica
Communication Solutions**
14, 15
Design Firm Hassenstein Design, Inc.

1. Client   Sunflower Music
    Designer   Monica Hsu

2. Client   Brooklyn IVF
    Designer   Monica Hsu

3. Client   Twenty-First Century Women
    Designer   Monica Hsu

4. Client   Wrenchead.com
    Designers   Joe Allen & Kerstin Hoera

5. Client   Brightidea.com
    Designer   Gregg Friedman

6. Client   Print Promotions, Inc.
    Designer   Stacey Geller

7. Client   Lead Dog Design
    Designers   Lucia Heffernan & Joe Allen

8. Client   Paramount Technologies
    Designer   Charles S. Trovato

9. Client   Woodland Park Zoo
    Designer   Craig Terrones

10. Client   Woodland Park Zoo
    Designers   Nino Yuniardi & Craig Terrones

11. Client   Woodland Park Zoo
    Designer   Craig Terrones

12. Client   Sirach
    Designer   Craig Terrones

13. Client   Innovant Corporation
    Designer   Craig Terrones

14. Client   Replay Records
    Designer   Susanne Hassenstein

15. Client   General Housewares Corp.
    Designer   Susanne Hassenstein

1.

2.

3.

4.

5.

6.

7.

1 - 4
Design Firm The Font Office Inc.
5 - 7
Design Firm Hassenstein Design, Inc.

1. Client   Stellar Management
    Designer   Charles S. Trovato

2. Client   Q-5 List Marketing
    Designer   Charles S. Trovato

3. Client   I-List Connection
    Designer   Charles S. Trovato

4. Client   PlusMedia
    Designer   Charles S. Trovato

5. Client   A & P Security Systems
    Designer   Susanne Hassenstein

6. Client   TriArch
    Designer   Susanne Hassenstein

7. Client   DDD Design
    Designer   Susanne Hassenstein

(opposite)
Design Firm   Hornall Anderson
                    Design Works

Client   Foster Pepper Shefelman
Designers   John Hornall, Julie Keenan,
                   Katha Dalton, & Nicole Bloss

1.

2.

3.

SUMMIT COMMUNICATION SERVICES, INC.

4.

5.

6.

7.

8.

9.

flexicore systems, inc.

10.

11.

12.

13.

14.

15.

1.

SQUARE HAÜS
DESIGN GROUP

2.

3.

4.

5.

6.

7.

8.

9.

10.

11. COMMUNITY COLLEGE

12.

13.

14.

15.

1
Design Firm Square Haus Design Group
2 - 12
Design Firm Rick Johnson & Co., Inc.
13 - 15
Design Firm Design Directions

1. Client   Square Haus Design Group
   Designer   Dion M. Isselhardt

2. Client   Deming Duck Race
   Designer   Mark Chamberlain

3. Client   Rio Grande Nature Center
   Designer   Mark Chamberlain

4. Client   New Mexico Optics
               Industry Association
   Designer   Mark Chamberlain

5. Client   Albuquerque Convention &
               Visitors Bureau
   Designer   Mark Chamberlain

6. Client   Double Tree Hotel
   Designer   Mark Chamberlain

7. Client   Susan B. Fomen Foundation
               of Central New Mexico
   Designer   Mark Chamberlain

8. Client   Suncare
   Designer   Mark Chamberlain

9. Client   Samaritan Institute
   Designer   Mark Chamberlain

10. Client   Fable
    Designer   Mark Chamberlain

11. Client   TUI
    Designer   Mark Chamberlain

12. Client   New Mexico
               Department of Tourism
    Designer   Mark Chamberlain
    Tin Work   Fred Lopez

13. Client   Leapdrog Marketing
    Designer   Melissa Muldoon

14. Client   Natural Creations
    Designer   Melissa Muldoon

15. Client   Family Centered
               Alternatives Counseling
    Designers Melissa Muldoon

363

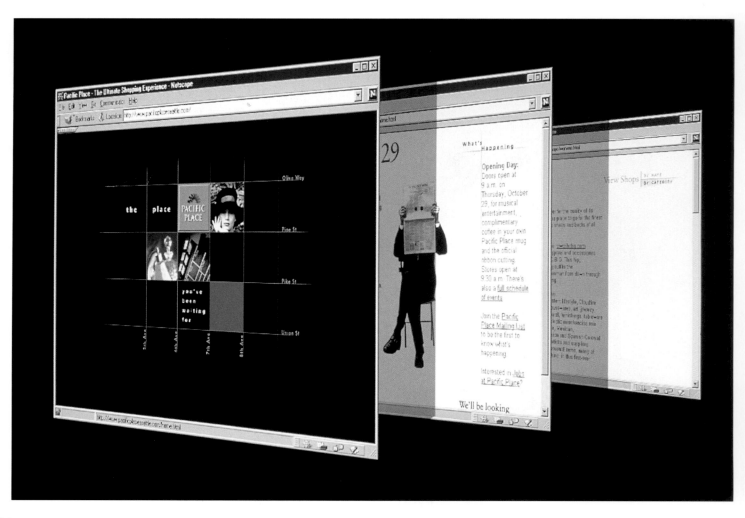

SUNFLOWER
HOLISTIC
Home Health Care, LLC

1.

HOPE
CHRISTIAN CHURCH

2.

Equity**Source**

Innovative Capital Creation

3.

4.

5.

6.

THE
FAMILY ARENA™

7.

(opposite)
Design Firm Hornall Anderson
Design Works

Client   Pacific Place
Designers   Jack Anderson, Heidi Favour,
& David Bates

1 - 3
Design Firm Design Directions
4 - 7
Design Firm Nova Creative Group Inc.

1. Client   Sunflower Holistic
Designer   Melissa Muldoon

2. Client   Hope Church
Designer   Melissa Muldoon

3. Client   Equity Source
Designer   Melissa Muldoon

4. Client   Hobart Welding Products
Designer   Tim O'Hare

5. Client   Hobart Welding Products
Designer   Tim O'Hare

6. Client   Hobart Welding Products
Designer   Tim O'Hare

7. Client   Family Arena
Management Enterprise
Designer   Dwayne Swormstedt

1.

2.

ALBUQUERQUE
RENEW
It's the Eco–*Logical* thing to do.

3.

SUNSHINE
Polishing Cloth

4.

5.

6.

7.

8.

9.

10.

11.

QUAIL RANCH
A natural way of life

12.

13.

14.

CHANNEL
105ONE fm
all hit music

15.

(all)

Design Firm Rick Johnson & Co.

1.	Client	Public Service Co. of New Mexico
	Designer	Lisa Graff
2.	Client	Giant Industries
	Designer	Molly Davis
	Illustrator	Brad Goodell
3.	Client	City of Albuquerque
	Designer	Tim McGrath
	Copywriter	Tim Pegors
4.	Client	Rio Grande
	Designer	Tim McGrath
5.	Client	New Mexico Economic Development
	Designer	Tim McGrath
6.	Client	Albuquerque International Sunport
	Designer	Lisa Graff
7.	Client	On-Site Solutions
	Designer	Tim McGrath

8.	Client	Media Dynamics
	Designer	Tim McGrath
9.	Client	Santa Ana Golf Club
	Designer	Tim McGrath
10.	Client	Gold Street Caffe
	Designer	Rick Gutierrez
11.	Client	Interactive Solutions, Inc.
	Designer	John Reams
12.	Client	Quail Ranch
	Designers	Tim McGrath & Lisa Graff
	Copywriter	Katie Duberry
13.	Client	Albuquerque Women's Resource Center
	Designer	Tim McGrath
14.	Client	New Mexico Museum of Natural History
	Designer	Tim McGrath
15.	Client	Simmons Radio Group
	Designer	Tim McGrath

LuckySurf.com

1.

2.

flair

3.

4.

vírtumundo

5.

NEXTPHASE

6.

7.

8.

9.

10.

1.

2.

3.

4.

AMERICAN COMPOSERS FORUM

5.

6.

7.

8.

9.

90TH ANNIVERSARY

10.

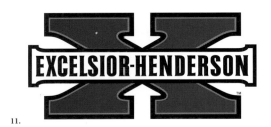

11.

12.

MINNESOTA STATE LOTTERY

13.

Field's Classic

MARSHALL FIELD'S TOURNAMENT OF LPGA CHAMPIONS

14.

15.

1 - 14				
Design Firm	**Foley Sackett, Inc.**			
15				
Design Firm	**Hornall Anderson Design Works**		8. Client	Foley Sackett, Inc.
			Designer	Michelle Willinganz
1. Client	American Composers Forum		9. Client	Foley Sackett, Inc.
Designer	Tim Moran		Designer	Michelle Willinganz
2. Client	Asia Grille		10. Client	W. A. Lang Co.
Designers	Michelle Willinganz & Joan Meath		Designer	Michelle Willinganz
3. Client	Cold Spring Granite		11. Client	Excelsior-Henderson Motorcycles
Designer	Chris Cortilet		Designer	Michelle Willinganz
4. Client	American Composers Forum		12. Client	Caterpillar
Designer	Tim Moran		Designer	Wayne Thompson
5. Client	American Composers Forum		13. Client	Minnesota State Lottery
Designer	Michelle Willinganz		Designer	Joan Meath
6. Client	Excelsior - Henderson Motorcycles		14. Client	Marshall Fields
Designers	Michelle Willinganz & Chris Cortilet		Designer	Michelle Willinganz
7. Client	Leeann Chin, Inc.		15. Client	IC2B
Designer	Chris Cortilet		Designers	Jack Anderson, Mary Chin Hutchison, & Andrew Smith

1.

2.

3.

4.

5.

6.

7.

8.

9.

10.

11.

Braunbach
Granite

12.

BLACK PEARL
PUBLISHING

13.

EPILOGUE
associates, inc.

14.

YOUR
RAPID-HIRE
SOLUTION

ACCELERATED
STAFFING

15.

1 - 5
**Design Firm Hornall Anderson
Design Works**
6 - 13
Design Firm Hallmark Levy Smith
14, 15
Design Firm White Communications, Inc.

1. Client   Hornall Anderson
                Design Works
    Designers   Jack Anderson & David Bates

2. Client   Onyx Corporation
    Designers   John Hornall, Debra
                McCloskey, Holly Finlayson,
                & Jana Wilson Esser

3. Client   Ground Zero
    Designers   Jack Anderson, Kathy Saito,
                Julie Lock, Ed Lee, Heidi
                Favour, & Virginia Le

4. Client   Anderson Pellet
    Designers   Jack Anderson & David Bates

5. Client   Space Needle
    Designers   Jack Anderson, Mary Hermes,
                Gretchen Cook, Julie Lock,
                Amy Fawcett, & Andrew Smith

6. Client   Mark Holtz
    Designer   Chuck Hodges

7. Client   FastPak
    Designer   Cesar Hallmark

8. Client   Thornhill Productions, Inc.
    Designer   Rick Levy

9. Client   Triad
    Designer   Rick Levy

10. Client   Dave Technology
    Designer   Rick Levy

11. Client   BeamLink
    Designers   Rick Levy

12. Client   Braunbach
    Designer   Sean Gregory

13. Client   Black Pearl
    Designer   Chuck Hodges

14. Client   Epilogue Associates, Inc.
    Designer   Karen B. White

15. Client   Executives Network, Inc.
    Designer   Karen B. White

1.

2.

3.

4.

5.

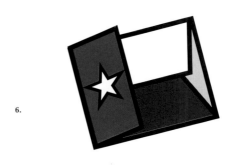

6.

Hallmark Levy Smith
Marketing & Creative, Inc.

7.

(opposite)		(all)	
Design Firm	**Hornall Anderson Design Works**		**Design Firm** **Hallmark Levy Smith**
Client	General Magic	1. Client	Sprouts Garden & Lawn, Inc.
Designers	Jack Anderson, Jana Nishi,	Designer	Cesar Hallmark
	Mary Chin Hutchison, Larry		
	Anderson, Michael Brugman,	2. Client	Gordon's Jewelry
	& Denise Weir	Designer	Chuck Hodges
		3. Client	Huge Image
		Designer	Cesar Hallmark
		4. Client	Sea Fresh
		Designer	J.R. Mounger
		5. Client	Nature Growers
		Designer	Cesar Hallmark
		6. Client	Paris Packaging
		Designers	Sean Gregory & Rick Levy
		7. Client	Hallmark Levy Smith
		Designers	Cesar Hallmark

1.

2.

3.

4.

5.

6.

7.

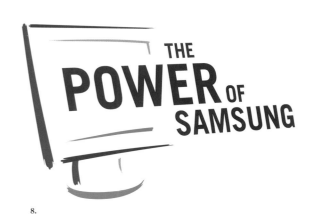

8.

9.

10.

11.

COLTON FIRST
BAPTIST CHURCH

12.

DAVID HOPKINS

PAINT & DRYWALL
INCORPORATED

13.

IRRIGATION
TECH

14.

Harlem Community
Development Corporation

15.

1, 2, 5, 8
    Design Firm   Muccino Design Group
3, 9
    Design Firm   Gray Cat Graphic Design
4, 7
    Design Firm   River Marketing, Inc.
6
    Design Firm   The Graphic Expression, Inc.
10, 12, 13
    Design Firm   P.K. Design
11, 14
    Design Firm   Fox Marketing
15
    Design Firm   Granola Graphics

1. Client   Koelling Communications
    Designers   Alfredo Muccino & Julia Held

2. Client   Last Minute Travel.com
    Designers   Alfredo Muccino &
                  Joshua Swanbeck

3. Client   Gray Cat Graphic Design
    Designer   Lisa Empleo

4. Client   River Marketing, Inc.
    Designer   Jennifer Sailer

5. Client   Affinia
    Designers   Alfredo Muccino, Michael
                  Lee, & Colm Sweetman

6. Client   ePatients.com

7. Client   Search International
    Designer   Jennifer Sailer

8. Client   Samsung Electronics
    Designer   Alfredo Muccino &
                  Joshua Swanbeck

9. Client   The California Clipper
    Designer   Lisa Empleo

10. Client   Lucia & Co.
    Designer   Phyllis Kates

11. Client   Fox Marketing

12. Client   CFB Church
    Designer   Phyllis Kates

13. Client   Hopkins Paint & Drywall
    Designer   Phyllis Kates

14. Client   Irrigation Tech.

15. Client   Harlem Community
                  Development Corp.
    Designer   Paul Howard

THE SUMMIT
AT SNOQUALMIE

1.

2.

workengine

3.

gettuit.com

4.

BURGERVILLE

5.

TECHNOLOGIES, INC.

6.

magicTalk™

7.

(all)
Design Firm Hornall Anderson Design Works

1. Client   The Summit at Snoqualmie
    Designers   Jack Anderson, David Bates,
                 & Sonja Max

2. Client   Hammerquist & Halverson
    Designers   Jack Anderson, & Mike Calkins

3. Client   Getuit.com "Workengine"
    Designers   Jack Anderson, Kathy Saito,
                 Gretchen Cook, James Tee,
                 Julie Lock, & Henry Yiu

4. Client   Getuit.com
    Designers   Jack Anderson, Margaret
                 Long, & Jason Hickner

5. Client   Burgerville
    Designers   John Hornall, Larry Anderson,
                 Bruce Branson-Meyer,
                 & Jana Nishi

6. Client   WatchGaurd
    Designers   Jack Anderson, Lisa Cerveny,
                 Mary Hermes, Kathy Saito,
                 Michael Brugman, Holly
                 Finlayson, & Belinda Bowling

7. Client   General Magic (MagicTalk)
    Designers   Jack Anderson, Jana Nishi,
                 Mary Chin Hutchison,
                 Larry Anderson, Michael
                 Brugman, & Denise Weir

(opposite)
    Client   Boullion Aviation Services
    Designers   Jack Anderson, Kathy Dalton,
                 Ryan Wilkerson, &
                 Belinda Bowling

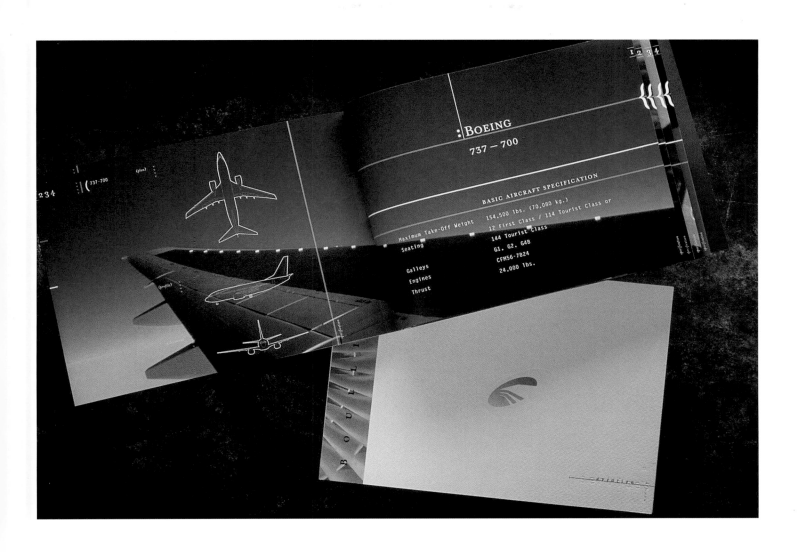

BOULLIOUN

Index

383

384